16 MARCH 2006
TO CARYL & JOHN
BEST WISHES D. M.

* INSCRIBED &
SIGNED BY
'RICK' (MATHER)

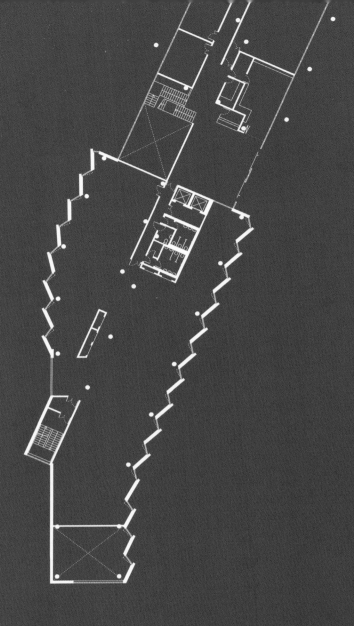

RICK MATHER ARCHITECTS

Robert Maxwell

Tim Macfarlane
Patrick Bellew

Black Dog Publishing

Contents

8 Deceptive Simplicity Robert Maxwell

16 Keble College, Oxford
24 Lincoln School of Architecture
30 University of Lincoln Masterplan
33 Hoffmann House
36 Neal's Yard Penthouse
40 The Priory
53 National Maritime Museum
62 The Wallace Collection
66 Royal Horticultural Society
72 Ashmolean Museum, Oxford
78 Dulwich Picture Gallery
86 University of Southampton Masterplan
92 Liverpool John Moores University Design Academy
96 Coking Works Masterplan, Chesterfield
98 South Bank Centre Masterplan
104 Virginia Museum of Fine Arts
110 Greenwich Landscape Masterplan
114 University of East Anglia, Norwich
128 Residential Quarter, Central Milton Keynes
131 Homes for the Future, Glasgow
134 The Times Newspaper Headquarters
138 ISMA Centre University of Reading
154 Urvois House
160 @venue Restaurant
164 Mirazur Restaurant, Côte d'Azur
166 Lyric Theatre
170 Eastbourne Cultural Centre

178 Optimising by Minimising Tim Macfarlane
196 Environmental Design Patrick Bellew
214 Timeline
228 Selected Bibliography, Colleagues and Consultants
238 Index

left: ARCO Building, Keble College, Oxford.
overleaf: Liverpool John Moores University Design Academy.

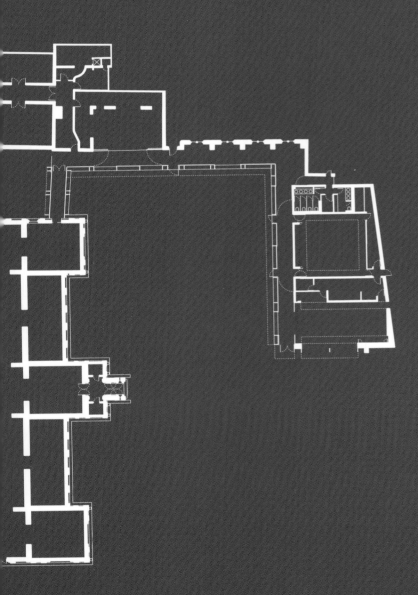

Deceptive Simplicity
Robert Maxwell

Why would a critic want to write a whole book about an architect? When I told Izi Metstein what I was doing, he snorted. Clearly, he thought I had in some sense sold out to a world of publicity, that I had sold my soul to the devil. Under his mild sarcasm I felt momentarily guilty. Why indeed had I put myself at another's service? My motives were not so simple. I did admire Mather's work; but I also had reservations, I liked some buildings more than others. Would this come out? Would I be forced to compromise?

When I visited the Lincoln School of Architecture, or the Priory in Hampstead, my feelings were unequivocal. I loved these buildings. In what follows I have kept close to the descriptions that these two visits brought out in me: what you felt at a particular moment is something in itself valuable that should not be discarded. When I visited the buildings at the University of East Anglia, my feelings were more mixed. I had always been sceptical of roof overhangs. So I confess there was an element of questioning. By agreeing to write a book I would force myself to conscientiously work through the whole body of work, and find out exactly where my reservations lay.

It would also be a useful discipline from another point of view. I had been dithering for some years over my 'next' book: let's face it, I had writer's block. Writing to a deadline

The Priory, Hampstead, London.

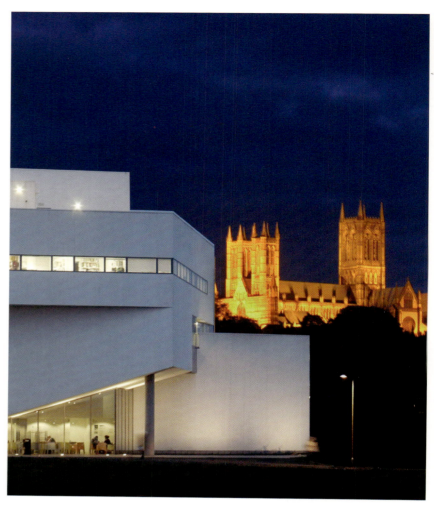

would get me out of that, or shame me into retirement. I would find out how consistent were my powers of criticism, how capable I was as a writer on architecture. So this was also a case of self discovery, never a bad thing if it leads to greater truth.

Although his work has developed to a distinguished level, Mather is an American, as his accent reveals. He holds two passports. With his planned work for the Virginia Museum of Fine Arts, he is on the verge of being recognised in the country of his birth.

Why would an American choose to live in London? Why would an American architect choose to live and work in Britain? The first question is probably unanswerable, but, somewhat to my surprise, there are indeed some who have made that choice, and have become successful. Within architecture, one thinks how much the Architectural Association owes to Alvin Boyarsky, a native of Montreal, who taught in Oregon. Today, the critic Charles Jencks comes to mind. He is not only a critic, but also an architect, a landscape designer, an artist, and an historian, with many publications to his credit, success in any country. There is of course a tradition of Americans who have made a life in Britain, starting with Henry James and TS Eliot, just as there is a tradition of Europeans who emigrated to Britain rather than to the United States, like

opposite: Lincoln School of Architecture. above: Oxford city centre. A variety of quadrangles and courtyards make up the colleges—a hidden world behind street-defining buildings. The practice's work at Keble College (top centre) contributes to this tradition by building around the Fellows' Garden to create the Newman Quad. At the Ashmolean Museum (left centre), part of the University, the practice is doubling display space on a constrained site, whilst retaining the original Grade I listed CR Cockerell building at the front.

Dirac and Gombrich. Obviously for Americans the language held in common has something to do with it, and English as a language to write in has a lot to offer anyone who has the urge to write. But if English has become a world language it is due to it having become the language of Americans. Although the idiom is different, it is still the same language. With the growth of estuary English, the difference in the way young people speak in the two countries is increasing, because both are living languages. But they still share the essential aspects of a common tongue, and given the realities of electronic communication, that is not likely to change.

As to why an architect should choose to live and work in Britain, we can begin to speculate. Britain is part of Europe, and shares, to a large extent, in the European respect for the old city. Double yellow lines and nationwide chains have begun to reduce the individuality of city centres, making for a dull uniformity. But in Britain, edge of town shopping centres are still competing with downtown, although under increasing restrictions, and the growth of pedestrianisation has contributed to this. Where streets have been pedestrianised, it is now possible to walk in these old centres and enjoy them as places, each one with its own special character. The city centre is still a goal. In both Oxford and Cambridge the University has virtually taken over the whole city, and the university quadrangles, where nature is tamed to the precision of a lawn, are more urban than rural in character. But even in the provincial cities, universities are still relatively close to city centres, and campuses have a certain urban and not only a rural character. In cities such as Warwick, ever since the authorities became aware of the lack of transportation for students, there are now bus services connecting student life to downtown.

In the United States, it sometimes seems as if the automobile has finally taken over. In Britain, there is more of a will to regulate its use. No American city has introduced a congestion charge, for instance, and it is hard to imagine that policy being brought to Manhattan. Indeed, London Mayor Ken Livingstone has been radical in that respect. A revolution in transport is still on the way, and in the meantime, we are faced with a certain mixture. A mixture of the new and the not-so-new. Could it be that this mixture offers to an American architect possibilities for design that are less available in the States?

I remember during my life in the States a conversation with an American friend who had spent a couple of weeks on vacation in Britain, and was thrilled with the experience. But, having recently arrived from London, I was puzzled: what was so good about it, I asked. She answered, "in England everything you see is genuine".

A slight exaggeration, yes, but you can see what she meant. The half timbered house fronts in Chester really are sixteenth century, the weavers' houses in Spitalfields, London, really are seventeenth century, the Burlington villa at Chiswick really is eighteenth century. And Pugin's Palace at Westminster, now restored and freshly gilded, is a vivid reminder of the period when London was about to rule an empire. A picture of it under construction shows it surrounded by low density suburban sprawl, making it hard to believe in the future that was about to happen. The history of the built environment in Britain stretches back for much longer than in the States— there is altogether more of the old left, and we are more used to working with what is already there. So for an architect who enjoys fitting in, there is a lot to offer.

And this seems to be an important element in Rick Mather Architects' work: the challenge of 'fitting in'. The prime effort of any architect is to be innovative, but there is a special challenge in being innovative without destroying what is already there.

Insofar as architecture is an art, it shares in many of the aspects that make art today. Art since Baudelaire has had to present itself as radical, and today has to lean forward into the future, and architecture is no exception. The development of Abstract and Conceptual work in the twentieth century has redefined what may be regarded as art. More and more it has come to be defined by the very fact of being offered for our contemplation in the art gallery or museum, so that we come to it with our attitude suitably composed. Yet the situation of any one building in the city does not automatically frame it as a work of art. However momentous it may be, it is found already embedded in the fixed context of the city, and already framed in the quotidian life of its inhabitants. For an individual, it can respond to a moment of emotion, as the spires of London did for Wordsworth when he contemplated the view from Westminster Bridge; or it can remain to all intents invisible, a mere background for the individual's routines or personal struggles.

Moreover, it is difficult to conceive of a city entirely made up of momentous events. It seems that for works of architecture to emerge as significant, they must be offset by a mass of building which does not speak out with silver bells, but remains most of the time mute and inglorious, a background to events, like Bloomsbury, or most of Bath. This is building that can be at best harmonious, but for the most part is commonplace. What then is the proper relationship between the commonplace and the special? How is architecture to be framed so that it can simultaneously be a background and a foreground? How is the city to be managed so that it belongs to everyone, yet can be appropriated by every individual during moments of personal epiphany?

This question recently provoked a debate between Vittorio Lampugnani and Daniel Libeskind, where Libeskind proclaimed the architect as the maker of the future, and

Lampugnani defended him as the father of the commonplace. No doubt both are right, but the circumstances of each case make it difficult to see who is right at any one time. Every architect, as a student, wishes to project himself against the best, and today, it seems, most architects are seeing themselves as students, and are taking the highest risk, and siding with the future, which they know is the winning side. There is now a widespread wish to be celebrated, to be a celebrity, like Frank Gehry, whose Bilbao has become the model of the means of regenerating a city. The wave of imitators has led Colin St John Wilson to condemn what he calls "icon architecture". For the architect who is trying to be the best, we wish him luck: but we know that most architects end up being thoroughly ordinary. It's a statistical certainty. In that case the attempt to make icon architecture every time will have led to error and pretentiousness. The process of renewal is not painless, and in his struggle with destiny the architect will not be aware of the threat he is making to the man in the street. The new with which the individual artist identifies, and with which he has already made himself familiar, has become his working environment, but it brings a threat to the common understanding.

There can be no easy answers within the essentially public art of architecture. As an art, architecture must admit to prior restraints, arising out of its place in the public realm. It can never be weightless, can never be totally abstract. It finds itself, as an art, uneasily placed between the freedom offered by abstraction, and the duty of representation—that is, of reflecting accepted conventions. Any artist who wishes to invent the future is free to do so; we don't have to see his pictures, listen to his music, recite his poems. But if he's an architect, we can't escape his buildings, we will see them every day. A special responsibility devolves on the architect.

Architecture, as a form of expression embodied in buildings, cannot be at every moment revolutionary. Built form has a certain inertia that prevents it from following surface ideas and fashionable trends. This is not to say that architecture is too slow a dancer to be able to contribute to the movement of culture, but that its state of being embodied embeds it in a complex phenomenology. Architecture must defer to the

Keble College Oxford

Following a winning competition entry in 1991, the initial proposal identified a number of potential sites within the grounds, offering a long-term development plan for Keble College. Two of these sites have now been built on to enclose a new quad, known as the Newman Quad.

Adjacent to the Grade I listed nineteenth century North Range by William Butterfield, the ARCO Building is located at the north end of the Newman Quad. The Sloane Robinson Building defines the western edge with the Butterfield dining hall completing the quad to the south. The new buildings continue the precedent of edge development helping to reinforce the street and define green space within.

above: Sloane Robinson Building, Keble College. The new building defines the western edge of the Newman Quad.
opposite: The ARCO Building (right) and Sloane Robinson Building (left) define the newly created Newman Quad. The ARCO Building uses its terrace as break-out areas for the adjacent seminar space while the Sloane Robinson Building's terrace serves its theatre space below.

social, but this does not mean that it must entirely succumb to convention. To keep it level with the challenges that arrive every day, we still must depend on the individual architect who will take a chance, risk opprobrium, and propose new things. There is no way of ensuring that this will happen at the rate that society can stand. What I suggest we need most is exceptional architects who wish to be out of the ordinary, but at the same time see no objection to the idea of addressing what is already there. That seems to be what Rick Mather Architects want to do. They seem to locate themselves in the zone where architecture makes public space, the zone where it is thoroughly acceptable, even familiar, a part of the everyday. Yet to that stable situation they naturally want to bring something different, something surprising, something fresh. And this something, it seems, will come out of the very details that each building depends on for its existence.

When asked to design a building for Keble College, we know from the start that we shall be under the shadow of William Butterfield: an architect very much of his time, who now impresses us with the power and precision of his details, above all in his handling of brickwork. So it is hardly surprising that in this context Rick Mather Architects should come to use bricks, and should wish to measure up to Butterfield

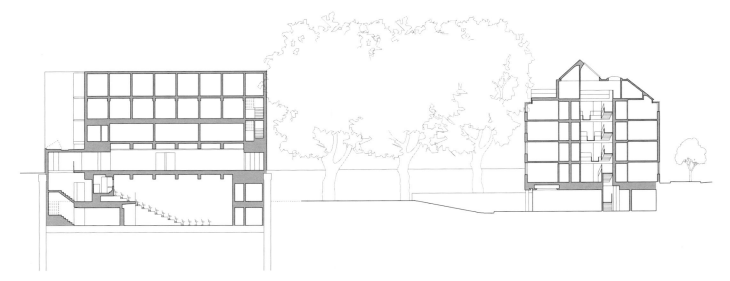

in the way they use them. The ARCO Building at Keble is located at the north-west corner of the college: rather than occupying the Garden, it draws back to the edge of the site, the better to contain it. There is no imitation of Butterfield's characteristic striped brickwork, but the brick chosen is an exact match in colour, and the materials of the room dividers on the top floor and the flower boxes that line the roof terrace exactly match Butterfield's slate roofs. With three rows of smallish windows, the building fits in to its surroundings without any fuss; yet the plan form and the exposed ground floor columns unequivocally proclaim its adherence to Modern Movement protocol.

And on the inside, the staircase goes beyond protocol to create an amazing sense of space: it takes its place beneath a roof light, so recreating on a small scale the equivalent of a Modern atrium. Its form is rather special: on each floor, a curved portion backing a curved wall, and a straight landing. But the straight landings diverge at a different angle on each level, gaining the attention, making an excitement, and creating a flow of space.

Not surprisingly, the architects were invited to do another building, and this also draws back to the boundary, so that the two together make the former Fellows' Garden into a quadrangle. This is the Sloane Robinson Building. Again, the exterior is the soul of discretion, although on the elevation to Blackhall Road it does comprise two *fenêtres en longueur*, and on the elevation to the garden the cylindrical columns now stretch

The 93 study bedrooms in the ARCO Building are organised into large flats over four storeys, each terminating with a shared kitchen/dining room facing south over the garden. The central staircase brings light into the centre of the plan and opens to a roof terrace at the top level. Seminar rooms at garden level open out to the south-facing terrace.

The largest feature of the Sloane Robinson Building is the 250 seat, flexible, multi-purpose O'Reilly Theatre. A dining hall and recital room are located at street level, while the upper floors contain six seminar rooms and 20 study bedrooms with views towards the Butterfield buildings and St Giles Chapel.

Both buildings employ low energy strategies, with the Sloane Robinson Building incorporating a unique geothermal ground water heating/cooling exchange system cast

above: Sections of the Sloane Robinson Building (left) and ARCO Building (right). The deep geo-thermal piles of the Sloane Robinson Building are clearly shown.
opposite: ARCO Building. Floor lights shine both up and down for maximum efficiency.

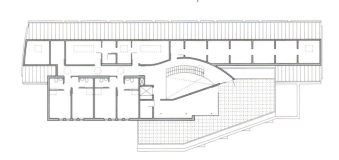

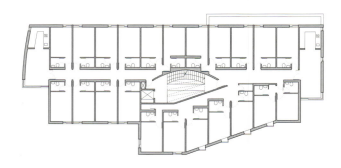

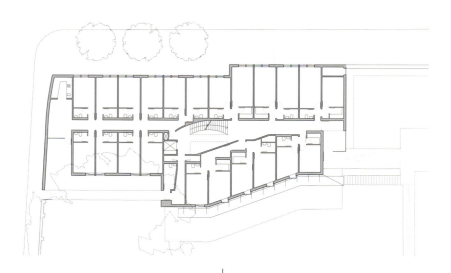

into the piles, the first of its kind in the UK. Buried pipes work to extract ground heat in winter for distribution through concrete slabs via a basement heat exchanger. In summer, the system is reversed to allow cooling. The electricity requirement of the system is around a third less than that used by conventional air-based systems.

Externally, reference is made to Butterfield's rich brickwork by the use of vertically and horizontally laid hand-made bricks that adopt a colour from Butterfield's polychromatic palette. On the Sloane Robinson Building to delineate the curved building ends the brickwork is vertically stack bonded, whereas the west elevation features a horizontal arrangement to complement the two inset glazed slots.

left: ARCO Building. Plans: top floor with two room flats; typical floor with two large flats; street level.
above: Sloane Robinson Building. From the staircase the Butterfield dining hall is framed by the new building.
opposite: ARCO Building, east entrance facade.

up through two floors to proclaim a certain grandeur, as well as allowing the space to drop downward between the street level and the theatre one floor down. Again, the staircase, constructed very elegantly in welded steel, is treated as an opportunity to make a flow of space up to the top light. The rounded forms of the landings emphasise the continuity, while making a sculptural statement.

Within a framework of fitting in, we are offered something that renews our enjoyment of Modernity. This works even with the matching brickwork, which consists of courses of narrow bricks laid vertically, so that they show themselves as a cladding material held on a concrete frame, not as structural brickwork standing up off the ground. The proprieties of an Oxford college have been maintained but the life that goes on in it has been lightened and brought closer to a younger generation.

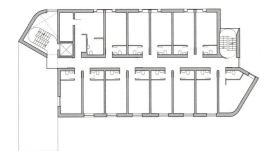

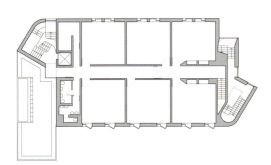

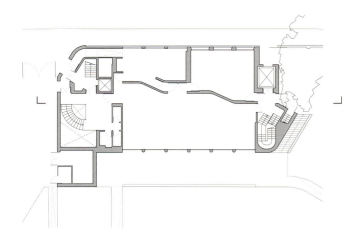

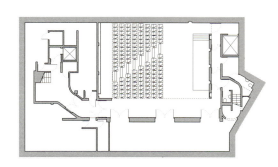

Sloane Robinson Building.
left: Plans: en suite bedrooms; seminar rooms; dining room and music room (above); flexible lecture theatre.
right: West elevation shutter (bottom right) opens for outside college access to the theatre.

Lincoln School of Architecture

The University of Lincoln School of Architecture is the first completed building in Phase One of the masterplan. As the first in a series of buildings that will establish the principles for future development, the School of Architecture is defined as much by elements yet to be realised as it is by existing site conditions.

Occupying a key site visible from all directions, the new School of Architecture has a strong sculptural presence while at the same time preserving and enhancing views back to the city. The east end of the building is cut back to reveal views up to the Cathedral on the skyline beyond.

A railway line runs through the campus defining the boundary of the site to the north. To the south the site borders the Delph Drain, a balancing pond for the nearby Brayford Pool that will be re-landscaped in the

opposite: Lincoln School of Architecture and Cathedral.
above: 'Lincoln c. 1802-3', by JMW Turner.

This is certainly true of the new School of Architecture for Lincoln University. It is a sober building that is a direct answer to the brief. But it is also a white-walled building, not only Modern, but looking like the kind of white-walled building that belonged to the heroic period of the 1920s. So it has an absolute purity, in contrast to the earlier recent buildings on campus, which are in a variety of materials, mostly brick. Or in contrast to the ancient building that stands for Lincoln on the world map: Lincoln Cathedral. Yet that contrast does not alienate the new building from its fellows, but increases its relevance. The architects have been conscious of the importance of the Cathedral and have worked to make its presence register on the daily life of the students below.

How have they done this? Not by creating a new kind of architecture, but by managing the familiar with a special finesse. The building is designed with economy in mind. More importantly, one can say that the search for economy has resulted in benefit. The school is a simple rectangle on a steel frame, with access off two parallel corridors. The space between the corridors has been expanded into an atrium that rises the full height of the building and pulls light down from above. This atrium is topped not in a glass roof, the cliché of our times, but in a series of skylights and clerestory windows. The light that comes down is not blinding, but filtered and reflected off the many white surfaces so that it has a magic quality of increasing the sense of spaciousness. And it does this without using up the budget. The space has been expanded by careful design, won by subjecting the brief to rigorous criticism.

The space of the entrance hall, for example, has been combined with the base of the atrium and the adjoining cafeteria to become the social centre of the building. It also provides the foyer to the two auditoria and the performance space at the west end of the building. The social spaces together form a sort of 'head' to the animal, and this not only animates the building, but the plan also. The auditoria are part of a game that puts into play angles that break the conscious rectangularity of the whole, and give a character to the end of the building that faces the city.

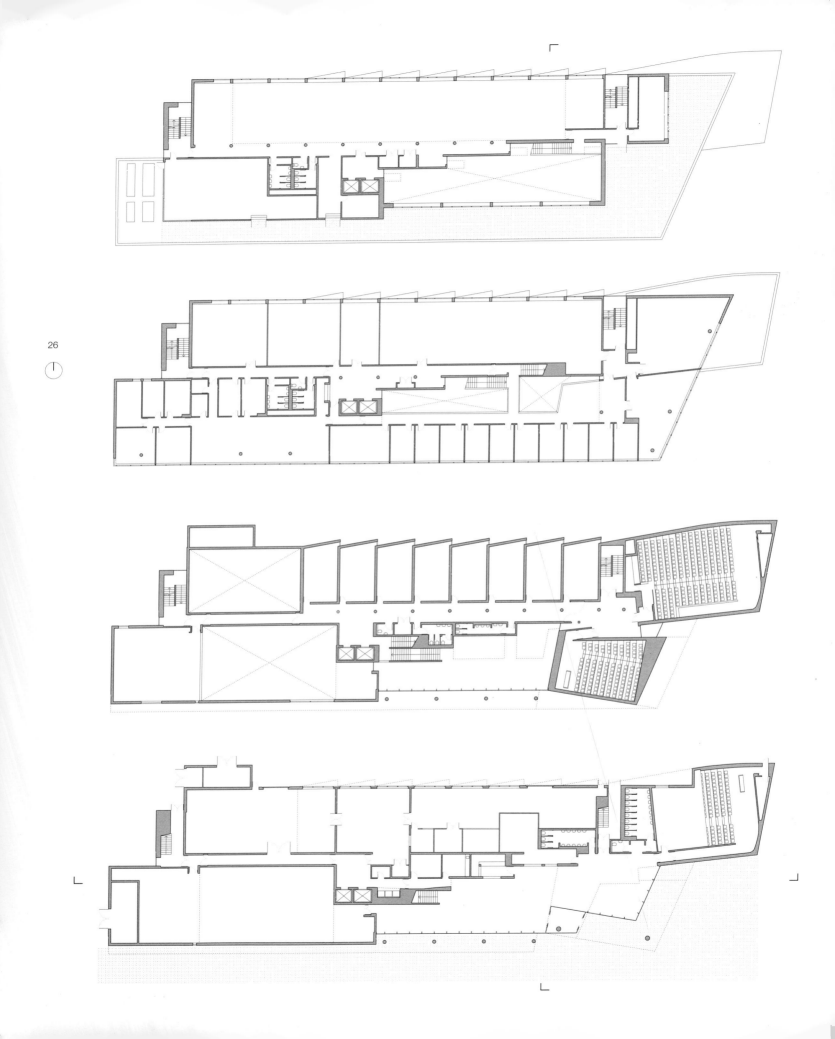

next phase of the masterplan to form a central water feature, a 'water square' around which future development will be focused.

The university's objectives were for a landmark building from a constrained budget, meeting academic requirements, which would signify the new campus, setting the standard for developments to follow.

Lincoln School of Architecture.
opposite: Plans: third floor studios and terraces; second floor studios and offices; mezzanine seminar rooms and lecture theatres; ground floor performance space and main lecture theatre.

These angles derive in the first place from the shapes of the auditoria. This is extended by slightly revolving them in relation to the axes of the main accommodation, accentuated by the glazing at the entrance. These changes are quite slight in the project as a whole, but they galvanise the volumes, and allow a constrained expression to come through. The climax of this movement is seen in the view north past the east end, looking to Lincoln Cathedral beyond. This opening forms a window through which campus and Cathedral are joined. In sunlight the shadow of the overhanging top floor comes to an exquisite point exactly on the south-east corner, which thus runs uninterrupted to the top of the building.

There is a further paradox here. To the critic, the detail is the source of interest; to the user, it is not of so much interest. Here, because it is everywhere consistent, it vanishes. The main architectural studio on the top floor runs the whole length and is lit by a south-facing clerestory, working with a one way pitched roof. Students from different years thus share space and environment, and are conscious of the whole into which they fit. At the east end there is an extensive roof terrace where you can take a break, or down a drink. Because there is, as it were, an absence of detail, there is no fuss, the building becomes the background to work.

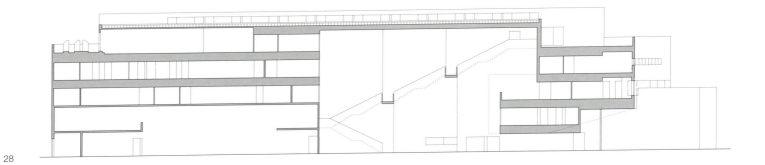

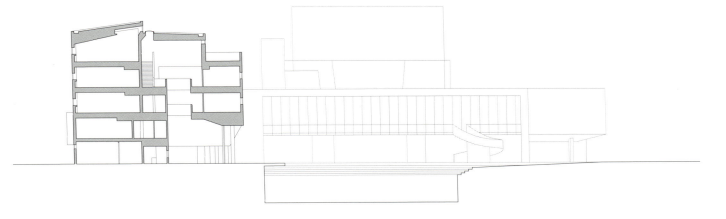

opposite above: Long section looking north.
opposite below: Top floor studio.
above: Cross-section through the pool with the Arts Centre in the background.
right: Atrium, looking down from the second floor.

It is, in sum, a discreet building, in spite of the all-out Modernism of its looks. It works first at being useful, then in looking good. It does not proclaim a unique vision, but it reinterprets Modernity in a unique way.

Rick Mather Architects have also prepared a masterplan for the campus as a whole. It will use peripheral buildings to exclude the doleful view to the superstores to the south, enlarging the site and its landscaped domain, providing new parking under trees, and focusing on a proper pool formed by shaping the balancing pond which keeps the water table stable in relation to Brayford Pool. In addition there will be a second Rick Mather Architects building, recently won in competition—the Lincoln Arts Centre—which will form a square together with the School of Architecture. This square will be a meeting place between Town and Gown. The masterplan also envisages new pedestrian links to the high street which leads uphill through the town centre, and beyond, to the Cathedral. There is thus a hope that the new intervention will go beyond its work on the site, and add significantly to the shape of the city itself.

The Arts Centre will be provided by the city, and it is a happy circumstance that its site will form part of the campus. It will be a major public building, incorporating a 750 seat theatre, two cinemas, an exhibition space and a cafe/bar/restaurant. By building it on campus, the city has shown a rare wisdom, for two sets of users, separately and together, will ensure a more regular use of the facilities, and will help to bring life to the public space across more of the day.

So far we have seen in one case a discreet use of brickwork; in another case a frank use of white render: materials are evidently chosen for their value in the environment. Except that there is at least one material that is chosen for its innate qualities: glass.

University of Lincoln Masterplan

The University of Lincoln's new Brayford Pool Campus will contribute to the regeneration of the city centre. The masterplan identifies key moves to capitalise upon the maximum impact in the short term without compromising later development. The strategy is to gradually connect this brownfield site to the urban fabric of Lincoln through the creation of a network of public spaces and animated routes, and to create a vibrant built environment that encourages partnering initiatives between the university and the city at large.

The masterplan establishes a strategy for the university's development, both short-term and long-term, to give the high quality built environment seen as key to the university's future success.

The 20 hectare (50 acre) riverside site next to the city centre has exceptional views across Brayford

above: Model of proposed masterplan, University of Lincoln.
opposite above: Section through Lincoln Arts Centre and pool.
opposite below: Lincoln city centre: showing new links to the high street (green) which then leads uphill to the Cathedral and Castle (site is red).

Pool to the Castle and Cathedral. Phased development exploits the full potential of the site. Phase One creates a central square to give maximum initial impact, with a sequence of buildings and routes linking to the surrounding city, giving the impression of a completed campus. The square features a pool redeveloped from an existing balancing pond to create a central landscaped feature to the campus.

Rick Mather Architects have also been appointed to design a new Arts Centre for the city on a site adjacent to the School of Architecture. The new Lincoln Arts Centre will be a major public building for the performing arts and media sited in the heart of the evolving campus.

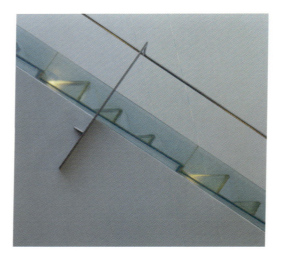 

Rick Mather Architects first came to public notice through designing restaurants, and I myself became aware of them through ZeNW3, my local Chinese restaurant, opened in 1985. It has a rivulet of water coursing down the double glass balustrade, which, it turns out, has for the Chinese a symbolic meaning. It is a pretty unusual use of glass, and it indicates Mather's interest in this material from the beginning.

But restaurants come and go, although ZeNW3 is still there. More effective in giving Rick Mather Architects the reputation of experts in the use of glass was a small extension to a house in Hampstead—the sort of minor extension that sole practitioners get to do all the time. The kitchen is re-organised, and a glazed verandah is added to the dining room, which became known as the 'all-glass extension'. Not only do we have large glass windows opening on to the garden, not only do we have a fully glazed roof admitting floods of light (even though north-facing), which improves the existing rooms; the beams that support that roof are also made of glass, delicately curved to emphasise their structural aspect, and they rest on glass beams. So it really is an all-glass building. The result is enchanting, and it may be said that the couple who carried it out in 1992 are still delighted with it, and enjoy it every day.

A daring use of glass, indeed: except that, as the engineer sees it, it is merely using glass within the limits of its strength. An engineer is essential for this kind of work, but not many engineers are given the chance to investigate the strength of glass: it was the architects' idea in the first place. It has now become part of their instinctive knowledge, as for example, in the use of glass balustrades to staircases and balconies. With Rick Mather Architects, the glass is not simply carried, it does the carrying.

above: ZeNW3, Hampstead.
opposite: Hoffmann House, Hampstead.

Hoffmann House
Hampstead

The first examples of all-glass construction, this house in Hampstead was remodelled to create greater interaction with its garden. The kitchen and dining area on the lower ground floor have been restructured to include a unique garden room constructed purely of laminated heated glass.

With no precedent for a structure of heated double glazed glass and a total lack of interest or skills from big UK glass manufacturers, the structural engineer, Tim Macfarlane, and builder Pat Carter, with Rick Mather Architects developed a completely new glazing system.

Roof and walls are formed by frameless double glazed panels with an invisible film that reflects heat, and conducts electricity. This generates radiant heat which is reflected into the building in winter, and solar gain out in summer, making it comfortable to use all year round. The panels are supported on three laminated glass beams and columns to make a completely transparent structure.

For the penthouse in Covent Garden, designed in 1993, Rick Mather Architects abandoned glass balustrades for a simpler combination of solid upstand and steel handrails: the effect is more spacious, in a tight and constrained plan, and with the upstands being white and sometimes curved in plan and the handrails being dark grey there are reminiscences of Le Corbusier's villa at Poissy, which is the building that most completely represents the Modern style. What is marvellous about this design is the clever way in which the various rooms have been dovetailed into a small irregular site, in such a way as to end up with a clearly orthogonal focus on the main window and its external terrace. It also employs fins on the roof garden, and 'smart' glass over the shower and master bedroom, all of which signal a special interest in the detail of design, a capability to make use of new materials. This reputation of 'taming' new materials indicates a willingness to use scientific know-how, and is more specific than a generalised adoption of the high tech style. This is professional competence at its most effective level.

Neal's Yard Penthouse Covent Garden

The site is in a quiet refuge in the centre of one of the liveliest areas of London. A large warehouse loft which had previously been dangerously converted (the roof was pushing the walls out and slowly collapsing) was stabilised and rebuilt into this 240 sqm (2,600 sqft) one bedroom apartment.

On the lower floor a series of cantilevered stair treads within a white space lead to the free-form plan of the upper floor. This large living space opens out onto two roof terraces. The double-height entrance dramatically links the two floors and brings light to the lower floor. The client's wish to be able to see the sky when he showered, and his roof garden upon waking, led to the inclusion of clear glass floors that change at the flick of a switch to translucent for privacy. Renovated and regularly spaced saw-tooth roof lights tie the irregular plan together and flood both levels with natural light.

Neal's Yard Penthouse.
left: The lower floor bathroom has views to the sky through the electro-chromatic glass in the ceiling.
opposite: The glass from above and the saw-tooth roof over the central stairwell.

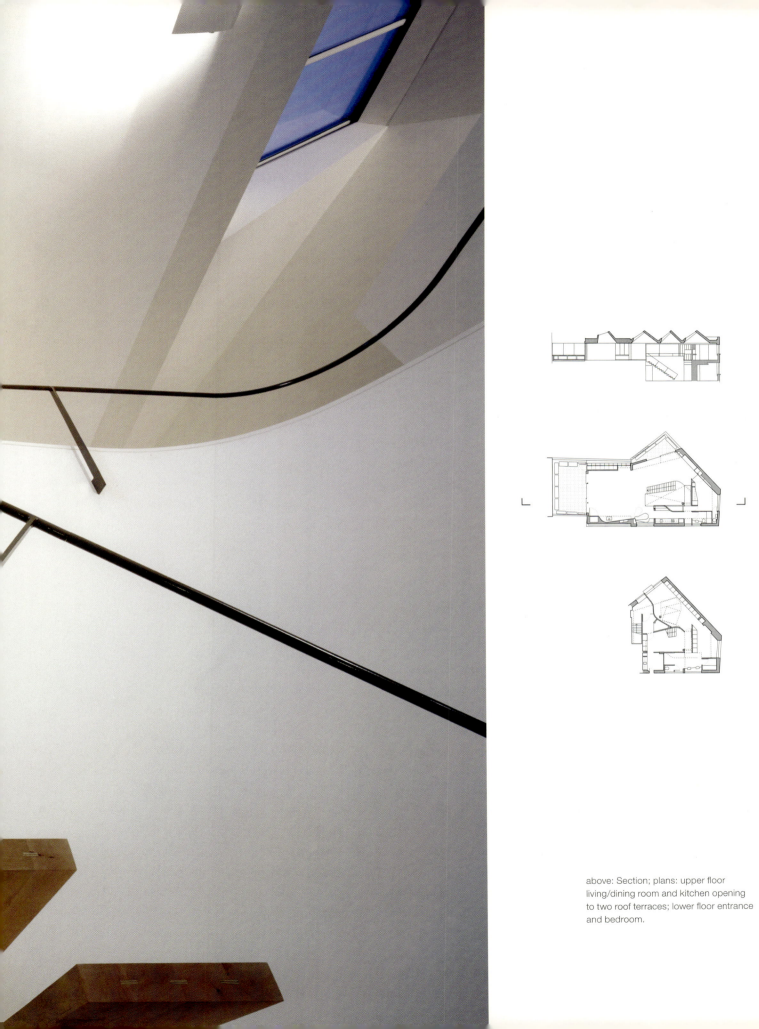

above: Section; plans: upper floor living/dining room and kitchen opening to two roof terraces; lower floor entrance and bedroom.

The Priory
Hampstead

This house adds to the tradition of Modernist villas in Hampstead, starting in the 1930s with houses by Maxwell Fry, Samuel & Harding and Connell, Ward & Lucas.

The site is at the top of Hampstead with views over London and the Heath. It was previously occupied by a 1950s four car garage with flats above and below. The surroundings are eighteenth and nineteenth century houses in brick and stucco; the planners had suggested only mock Georgian would be acceptable but eventually the completely modern design was given permission, endorsed by the neighbours and the influential Old Heath and Hampstead Society.

The three-storey dwelling opens up to roof terraces and down to the two levels of garden. Inside, the three levels interconnect through the double-height rooflit living space and down through the glass floor to the indoor swimming pool. A glass

The Priory, Hampstead.
opposite: Garden view.
above: Street view.

There is a house in Hampstead, known as The Priory, where the practice have again taken pleasure in a nuanced use of glass. This is a white-walled villa in the classical tradition: Modern, but orderly. Seeking it, there is no doubt when one has found it—it has a presence: a good deal of calm white wall, with limited openings judiciously placed; a corner window without glazing bars or corner mullion. The horizontal glass porch roof and vertical roof terrace screens give a hint of power in reserve, but there is nothing roguish about the effect. Seen from the road it presents a modest two-storey mass, set back a full house width from the street, screened by a high wall and fence. To the rear, the three-storey garden side towards the falling ground is virtually invisible. Externally it suits its environment perfectly: there are plenty of other white walls in this area, some are modern villas, even famous ones, and some are Arts and Crafts, *fin de siècle* and Georgian houses: no cause for alarm.

Internally, it is altogether not your ordinary interior—in effect sensational, and sensational because it engages actively with the senses. There is a swimming pool in the lowest floor, and its presence is evident from all the other levels because the living room floor incorporates at key points windows that allow you to look down on it. I say windows, but they are transparent sections of the floor that can be walked upon if you are feeling brave. Some parts of the house have voids that extend right up to the roof, so there is a play of space. Above all, if only because of the pool, there is a play of light. At the time of my visit we were under the regime of the standard overcast northern sky, but there was still this sense of light coming at you from all sides. In brilliant sunlight, the effect must be spectacular.

This is Modernism in the tradition of Modernism, owing a debt to the classic villas of Le Corbusier. Although horizontal sheets of plate glass are used to seal off the immediate pool environment, the space rises vertically from the lowest to the highest levels. The flow of space through all three storeys creates a sense of sculptural intention. Or, looking at it the other way, the space gradient runs downhill from the entrance on the middle level to the garden outlet at the far end of the pool, but this frontality is countered by the movement at right angles that flows from the study area

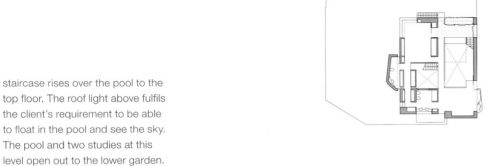

staircase rises over the pool to the top floor. The roof light above fulfils the client's requirement to be able to float in the pool and see the sky. The pool and two studies at this level open out to the lower garden. Views from the house are carefully controlled by the placement of the windows, translucent screens and landscaping to 'edit out' surrounding houses.

Structural glass is used extensively throughout the house; in the large roof light over the double-height living space, glass flooring, stair treads and risers, balustrading and external lay lights (which allow light from the garden level to illuminate the front facade), and in a glass 'slot' which runs between the main house and the front extension.

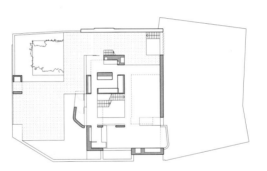

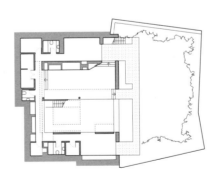

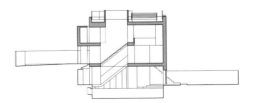

Plans: roof terrace; top floor; street level; garden level; section.

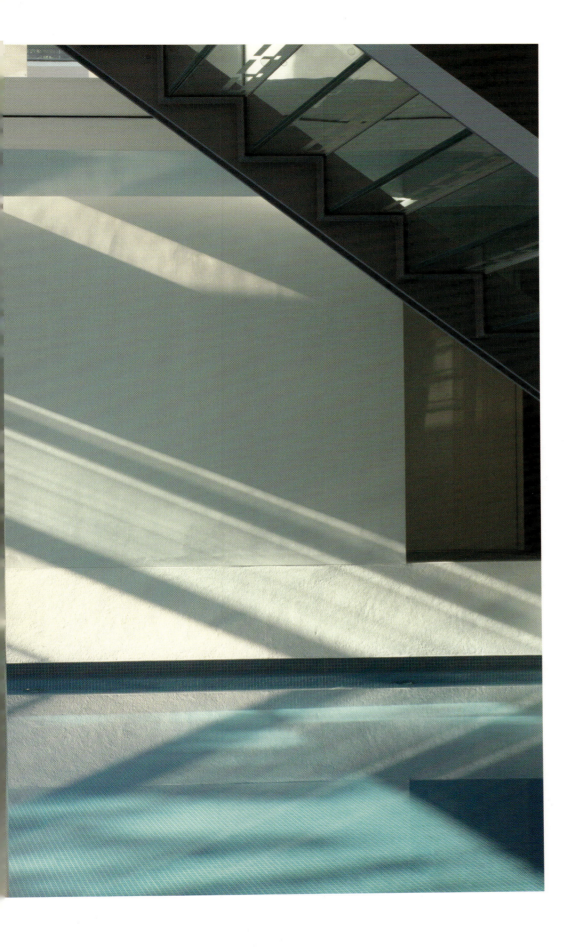

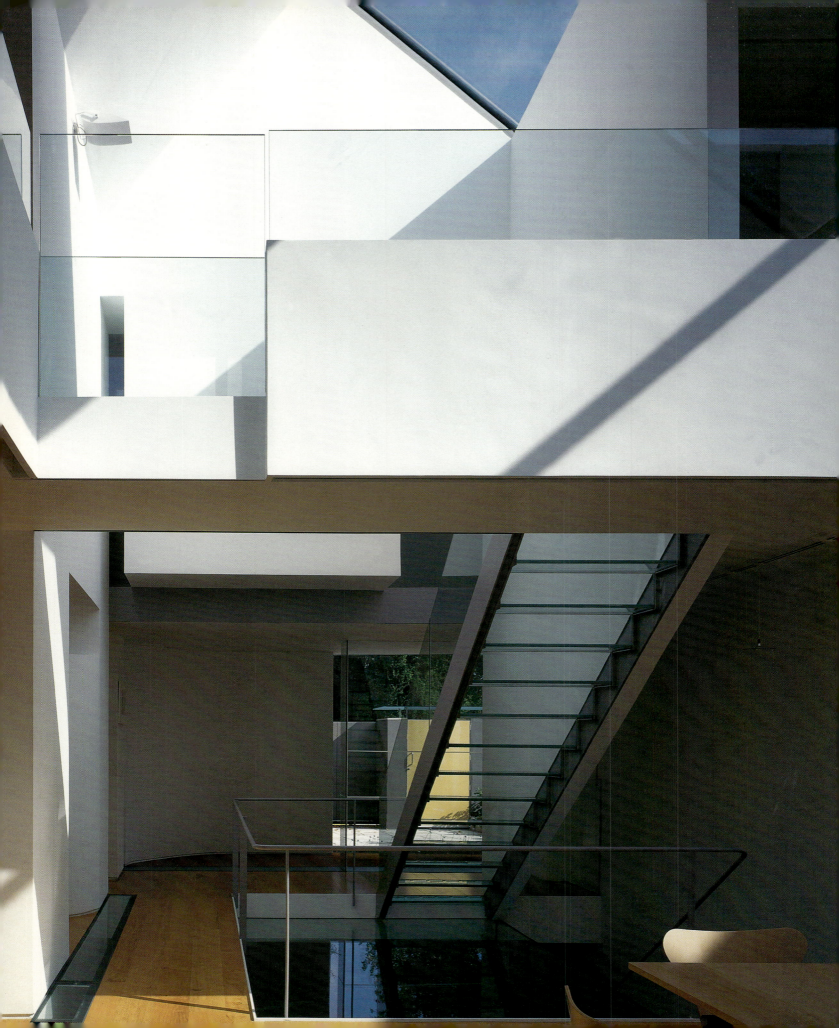

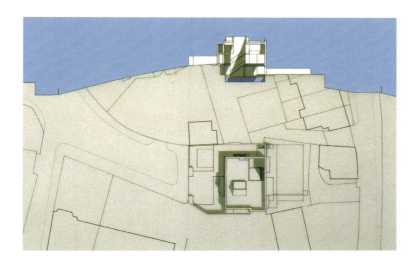

on the top floor down to the garden terrace outside the dining room, which is further emphasised by the main window—a roof light facing south and protected by an external blind—that again re-states the historical link with the artists' studios of Paris that first ventured into big windows. But the combination of two gradients crossing each other already expresses an evolved concept of space, as complex as we find anywhere in Le Corbusier. To this we must add a different, less classical, sense of materiality: the use of glass, whether horizontal or vertical, whether transparent or mirrored, creates a sort of blur, an uncertainty about limits that makes the final outcome very different from the inherited models.

There is certainly a very Corbusian moment when we stand on the little balcony off the study area and look back into the body of the house. From this point the spatial composition opens up in all directions, and one is positively glad of the anchor provided by the blank panel that screens the bedroom corridor directly opposite. This projects into the well (to provide cupboard space in the corridor) in a way highly reminiscent of the way the roof terrace projects into the upper part of the living room in the Maison Cook, 1926, by way of a segmental blank wall. In both cases, a sculptural mass works to stabilise the spatial flow.

However, nowhere in Le Corbusier do we find the play of narrow slots of glazing introduced to clarify the massing and the limits of the masses. This is more to do with Postmodern angst and the search for conceptual clarity. For example, the projection that encloses the entrance hall at ground level, and the shower room above it, is separated from the main volume by such a slot, requiring that the bather passes momentarily through a visible zone before reaching the privacy of the shower. It's no surprise to find that the owner has insisted on this glass being etched. Yet the slot still works to make one aware of the spatial hierarchy.

The aesthetic effect is further destabilised by the play of light, whether directly entering or reflected upward from the pool. The upper edges of the plate glass balcony fronts slice into the air, threatening as well as reassuring, blurring contours with their

preceding page: Garden level swimming pool.
opposite: View to the entrance.
above: Composite plan and section showing hilltop site and link between the pool and sky.

reflections while defining them physically with surgical precision. The glass treads to all the stairs draw attention to our movement as a poetic, sculptural promenade rather than as a practical motion. What will it be like when these conditions have become so familiar that one can run downstairs two steps at a time?

Even without sun glitter, even when all is still, the horizontal planes of glass and the pool itself create diagonals by means of the reflections they produce of the stairs, suggesting an Escher-like ambiguity, recreating a hunger for n-dimensional geometry, the desire to escape from gravity, an invocation perhaps of Lissitzky's call for "floating structures", his anticipation of a "physical-dynamic architecture" requiring "the conquest of gravity". This is part of today's climate, our wish to extend from real limits into artificial ones that we ourselves choose, like the desire for cyber-space.

If these remarks lean towards formal criticism, this is not to suggest that the architects have floated away from their task. Mather was chosen out of five architects interviewed, and his sketch solution to a complex brief was instantly accepted. The client clearly wanted a house which would go beyond mere convenience and become in its own right a work of art. At the same time it is laid out with a great practicality, for example in separating the two single bed-studies into corners in the ground floor where they are virtually removed from the spatial drama of the main house, so making them good for guests or grandchildren. It is wonderfully sensitive to the immediate outside prospect, so that the main windows are directed at the best and most idyllic views, and the walls as well as moulding a dynamic space also hide the adjacent buildings. In this respect the building is an object lesson in showing what is lost by the Miesian approach of opening up all the elevations on all sides, and how screening by walls is so much more convincing than screening by flimsy Venetian blinds. In addition, the space of corridors and cupboards is on an ample scale, allowing on occasion a swift transition from domestic squalor to pristine display.

By eschewing the provision of covered garages, the front and back gardens are made into coherent spaces that define the domain of the villa, giving a paved herb

The roof terrace screen frames views and prevents overlooking.

garden on the public side and a classic lawn-under-trees on the other. There is a generous provision of sitting out space adjacent to all the main functions, so that the outside is immediately available whenever the sun shines. From the lawn, the south-west elevation is an end in itself: stabilised by the recess where the pool reaches the outside, activated by the asymmetrical play between the remaining windows, it fulfils in ampler form the promise of the entrance side. The house is full of light, but from all sides, competing in a complex and enjoyable dance: a great place to live, and an impressive piece of architecture.

How this has come about is something of a mystery: it's Mather's secret. On the other hand, it may also be due to a certain sense of architecture as a craft, something with clear boundaries, something that you can learn to do. In that sense it is inseparable from the way that you do it: it comes out of the detail. Architecture exists already before Mather comes to it, and if he brings something to it, it doesn't change its essence. Clearly, this is very different from the way a Libeskind, or an Eisenman, looks at it. The world, in their view, is privileged to enjoy their vision.

Recently, during a speech at the RIBA, Peter Eisenman told how he was looking down at the new centre at Compostela with his client, when the client asked: "but what will this space be for?" Peter said, "I had a sudden inspiration, I said: 'it's for the air-conditioning'". It would not be possible for Mather to improvise in this way, because by the time he is looking in with his client, he has been through all the possibilities. Whereas Peter Eisenman starts with a wild and accidental plethora of forms, on which he then works to make sense, Mather starts with the brief, and he knows it intimately before he makes the key design decisions. But where does chance come from, which in Eisenman is the main source of the unexpected? When asked this, Mather said, "the brief and the site are full of chance and the unexpected, all you could want, all I need". That gives you, in a nutshell, his attitude towards architecture.

It is not just the choice of building materials, obviously: more to do with the way they are chosen in combination, how they work in context, how their surfaces absorb or reflect light, how the effect of using them together builds a total sensation. There has to be this materiality, I believe, as the kind of base substance out of which the architectural sensation can grow. But this does not preclude access to the upper reaches of architecture, its appeal to the intellect, to the sense of history. With an architect like Rem Koolhaas, we seem to start with this, and work down to a series of shock sensations, which can certainly be salutary. With Mather, we start with the known, and we end by skirting the unknown. The interest in building materials is something that has produced an openness towards the brief, and out of that comes a variety of results, so that there is also a variety of styles; but not a feeling that the style was chosen first, or arbitrarily.

This result is very different from that achieved by many other architects, where the choice of style appears to express an ideological commitment. There, the ideological position becomes locked into a personal choice of building form that is used like a signature. Richard Meier has learned the white-walled style, and if we choose him, we get that. Morphosis now seem to stand for the deconstructive style; you choose them in order to get that. Gehry's style is personal—if you choose him, you get him. But Mather does not stand for a style. If we choose him, we don't know what we will get. It is something that will make its way into existence step by step, as the architect works to absorb the brief, to put everything into context, to bring many things together. The idea of following the function has produced a very open result: a building that not only works for the client, but that is also a source of surprise and interest, and even of the unexpected. Some of that comes from the brief, undoubtedly, but some must be due to the architect's own sensibility, his feelings not only for materials but for architectural meaning.

One of the areas in which this approach seems to pay dividends is the updating and improvement of a building already familiar to the general public. Rick Mather Architects have been especially successful in this. Here the approach is natural; it stands to reason that the result will incorporate what was already there, since the object is to ameliorate its use.

The earliest example of this is their work at the Architectural Association. Three Georgian houses, run together, still full of mouldings, still a gracious environment in spite of the rackety life of the students, and their propensity to introduce shocking, if temporary, innovations. There, the architects dealt with structural problems in the old building, cleaned out walls that could be demolished, created the slide library, made more connections to the studios behind, and improved the reception area, the dining room, the exhibition hall: but most notably, they reinstalled the bar. The bar is the meeting place, the centre of life for a building that works itself as a social hub. The bar has been designed with two cupboard doors that open out to display the bottles, so that it looks neat whether it is open or closed. The mirrors placed at right angles below the curved corners of the counter give a floating effect; it's only when you are sitting low down opposite them that you notice your own reflection and see how they work to show you lifting your right arm, the arm you have just raised, not the mirror opposite arm. So there is wit along with superb aesthetics.

The main examples of their work with old, sometimes venerable buildings, are the National Maritime Museum at Greenwich, the courtyard at the Wallace Collection, the main hall at the Royal Horticultural Society, the Natural History Museum in Kensington, the Ashmolean at Oxford and Dulwich Picture Gallery. None of these cases would have come about were it not for an initial discussion between client and architects, which generated interest, yes, but more importantly, trust. There will have been

above: The Architectural Association bar.
opposite: The National Maritime Museum, Greenwich, from the street.

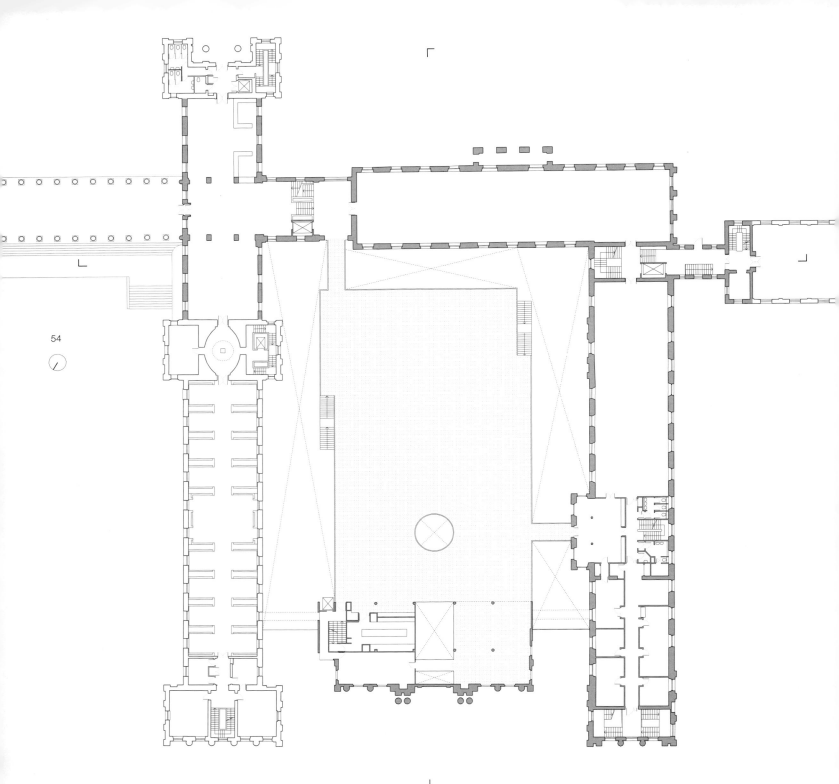

54

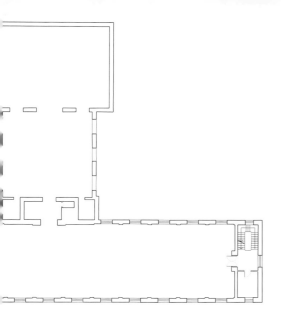

National Maritime Museum, Greenwich

The courtyard is covered with a freespan glazed roof over a new, raised central 'square'. The podium level of the square creates 'streets' along the base of the courtyard facades. Stairs against the podium link the 'streets' with the new square. Within the surrounding building, ten new galleries were created and all levels are now fully accessible.

Bridges link to the surrounding galleries and new stairs and lifts at the corners link the different levels of galleries together, allowing the visitor to move continuously throughout the space.

an understanding by the architects of the immediate and long-term needs of the institution, so that the client is not merely provided with an immediate solution, but with a long-term strategy for the future. This kind of work leads to another kind: the preparation of a masterplan for an entire site, and Rick Mather Architects have been very successful in that kind of work too.

The National Maritime Museum is probably the most visited of these. Its proximity to the Cutty Sark and the presence nearby of a river-bus pier, as well as the Docklands Light Railway, all ensure that it is on the tourist route, as much for people from the UK being patriotic about the Navy, as for people from abroad. And, of course, like the National Gallery, it is free. So thousands have entered, and have been wowed by the main space. What was at one time an open court, is now an enclosed area with new gallery space, a reception, shop, lifts and other services. These facilities occupy the ground floor. Above them is a flat floor, paved in stone and largely empty, which extends beneath the new glazed roof. This is currently the largest freespan glazed roof in Europe. It makes a new space, and it is stupendous. The platform stops short of the containing volume on all four sides. It contains a restaurant, and the seating for it, and three large showcases full of exhibits. Less visible is the initial work carried out to

National Maritime Museum. Podium level plan. Lutyens created the library in the north-east wing when the building was converted to a museum in the 1930s.

The National Maritime Museum framed by the towers of the Chapel and the Painted Hall of the Old Royal Naval College by Christopher Wren and Nicholas Hawksmoor. It is connected to Inigo Jones' Queen's House by the colonnade.

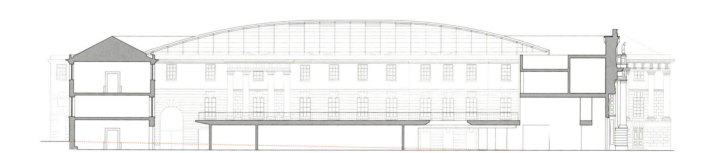

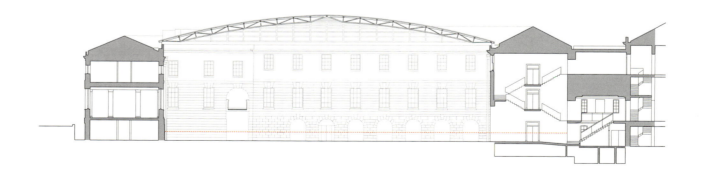

The project removed courtyard additions to Sir Philip Hardwick's original scheme and reveals, refurbishes, and restores the grandeur of the original Neo-classical facades.

The existing triumphal arch of the north facade is reinstated as the main entrance. Internally it has been expanded to provide new galleries, shop and reception area. A new glass lift provides views over the glazed courtyard.

make for freer access, by clearing out the corners of the plan and inserting new stairs and lifts. So far as the running of the building is concerned we have gained a service floor and a new major viewing gallery, and regained the courtyard, without the rain which so often made it unusable.

What the public may not notice, although it is there for all to see, is the exact way that the new roof has been executed. It is not simply a shed roof, where all the trusses run in parallel, one after the other, in sequence. Because the courtyard was square in plan, diagonals have been provided, so that the roof is effectively hipped, and the span is reduced to four quarters, leaning together to make a pyramid. This makes the open structural trusses less obvious, and contributes to the feeling that the roof has always been there.

opposite above and above: Construction sequence: April 1997; October 1997; February 1998; March 1998.
opposite middle: North-south section through podium and triumphal arch (red lines indicate previous ground level).
opposite below: East-west section through southern 'street'.
overleaf: Views to the entrance under the podium and in to the western 'street'.

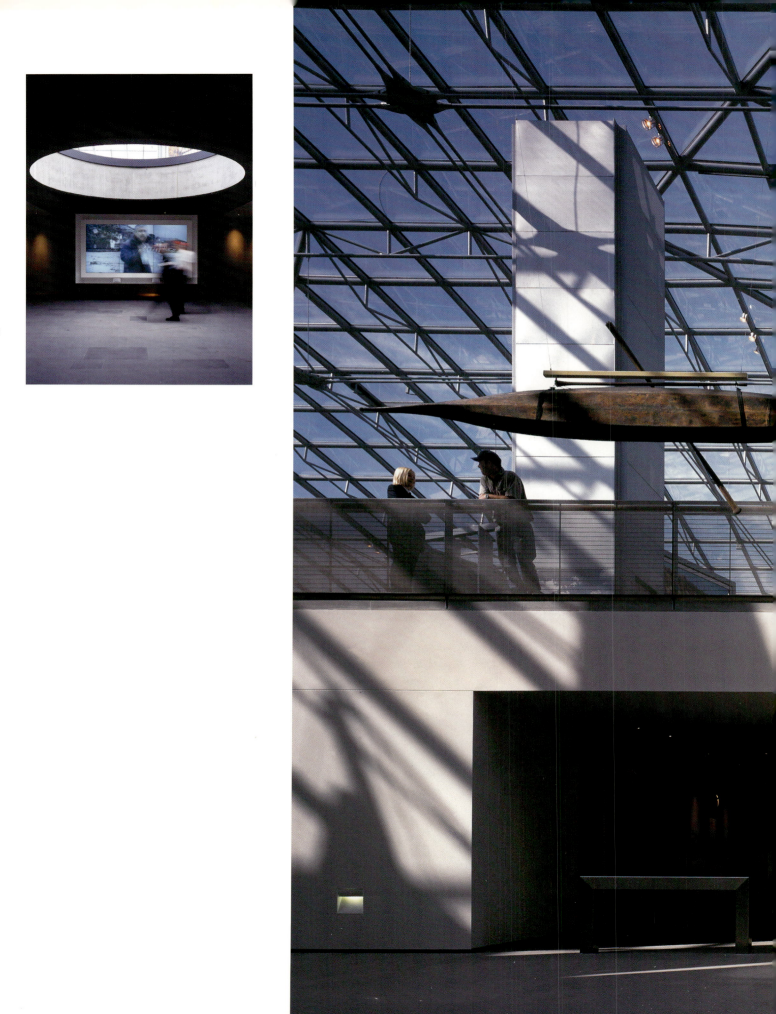

The Wallace Collection also has a square courtyard, and again the architects have enclosed it with a glazed roof, divided into four quarters. There was a difficulty, however, since one side is a storey higher than the other three. Their solution was direct. The quarter of roof on that side tilts the other way, so that the eaves rise to enclose the top storey, which is thus not excluded from the new space. The difference between the two adjacent quarters is filled with a vertical glass wall. The result is not particularly elegant, but it is not something that you notice, so quietly is it done. For a time, I worried about it, went back to view it again, and decided it was the only practical way to solve the problem. The use of the courtyard has relieved the congestion of what is otherwise a group of separate rooms, and makes the building doubly enjoyable for the visitor.

The paved courtyard runs to the elevations on three sides; the fourth is separated by a balustrade, on a curve, and this space has been used to provide a staircase down to the lower gallery floor, symmetrically on either side of the main axis. The staircase is supported only on one side, with solid risers that form a continuous serrated mass.

The Wallace Collection

Hertford House houses The Wallace Collection and was built as Manchester House in 1776–1788 for the Fourth Duke of Manchester. The Wallace Collection was opened to the public on 22 June 1900 by the Prince of Wales, and Prince Charles, the present Prince of Wales, opened this project exactly 100 years later. The collection is known above all for its French eighteenth century paintings, Sèvres porcelain, and European and Oriental arms and armour.

The scheme was won in a limited competition in 1995 for its Centenary Project, the last chance to expand the gallery within the existing fabric (on its landlocked site), and consequently safeguard the collection's physical and financial future. The expansion enables the display of the entire (static) collection, improved educational, library and archive facilities, and the new courtyard restaurant.

The Wallace Collection.
above: Red lines denote the extent of the new excavation.
left: The island nature of the site dictated the strategy for expansion (taken before the glass roof over the courtyard was built).

To achieve the client's goals, the entire basement was excavated below the courtyard and rear galleries, the courtyard was glazed over to provide a Sculpture Court and restaurant, and the original basement was renovated and re-planned.

The whole museum had to be underpinned for excavation. The existing galleries above, with their priceless collections, remained open to the public throughout the entire construction period. The work more than doubles the area in the basement and provides new exhibition galleries.

The hitherto unseen Study and Fakes Reserve Collections are now on public view, displayed in a series of galleries that extend into the original museum's vaults under the street. There is also a temporary exhibitions gallery; a gallery to display the

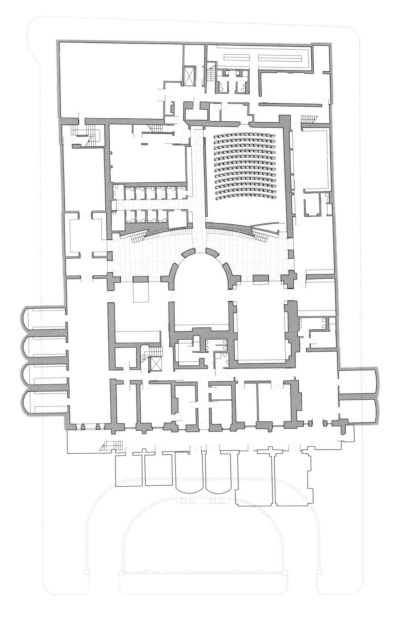

Basement plan. The area north of the curved bay is newly created by the excavation.

Wallace's collection of watercolours and miniatures, an extensive archive space and the museum library.

New glass and pre-cast stone stairs connect the enlarged lower courtyard to the main level. The upper courtyard was covered with a lightweight steel and glass roof (manufactured in Prague) which enabled the creation of a Sculpture Court and restaurant, now the central focus of the whole building. This provides greater accessibility to the surrounding gallery spaces. The successful new restaurant has zinc-clad waiter stations, with a bar concealing the dumbwaiters which rise discreetly from the new kitchen below.

Trees provide shade in this internal room. Environmental control is achieved by natural ventilation with automatically opening vents at eaves level. Heating and cooling are from pipes embedded in the new Portland stone courtyard floor.

opposite: New stair links the original courtyard level to the expanded basement.
right above: One side of the pyramidal roof is raised to accomodate the higher south facade.
right below: Excavating the courtyard.

Royal Horticultural Society

This extensive redevelopment of the Royal Horticultural Society's (RHS) Headquarters building in Vincent Square provides a new home for the Lindley Library, offices and an entirely remodelled conference hall facility. Listed and dating back to the early 1900s, the building has been extended into hitherto unexploited basement areas and comprehensively refurbished to house the library's growth over the next 25 years.

The Lindley Library is one of the most important botanical reference libraries in the world and consists of over 50,000 volumes covering a wide range of subjects, including garden history, botany, flower arrangement, and botanical art. It is used by scholars from all over the world. It is also much used as a resource by garden writers, authors, and members of the general public to whom it is freely available.

The RHS thought that there was not room to house the Lindley Library in their existing building and it would have to be moved out of London to the RHS gardens at Wisley in Surrey. The new masterplan demonstrated that by excavating the basement to a useable depth, extending out into the front area, re-planning and

some rebuilding it was possible to house the library and other pressing needs, and to cover the RHS' future requirements, in their existing Headquarters, without moving.

Leaving the library in London meant that it could continue to be of easy access to anyone by public transport and straightforward for foreign visitors and scholars to find.

From the ground floor library reception and reading room, with views over Vincent Square, a new glass and steel stair leads down to the lower library. It is naturally lit through large roof lights offering views up to the surrounding trees. The library is serviced with modern environmental control, including sophisticated fire and flood protection systems for the collection. The new basement also accommodates extensive archive space, conservation facilities and staff work areas.

Royal Horticultural Society.
opposite: Refurbished Elverton Street elevation, now the main entrance to the hall, seamlessly added to the old design.
above: RHS, 1904, before an extra storey was added in the 1930s to accommodate the Lindley Library, now relocated.

There are two stainless steel handrails—the one on the outside supported on glass panels which are fixed to the side of the steps, each piece accompanying six steps. Look how the lower edge of the glass is cut, two steps at a time, to see Mather's instinct for material.

At the Royal Horticultural Society's Headquarters Rick Mather Architects have moved the Lindley Library from the top to the newly excavated basement floor. Here, too, there is an elegant staircase down to the main library floor. The stainless steel handrail is again supported by a glass balustrade, itself supported from a continuous steel edge to the steps. The reading rooms below ground level hardly suffer, because of two glass roofs, used above the main reading space and offices, one on either side of the front door, which provide ample light. These spaces are not tall—the glass roofs are just a few feet above your head—but protected by a stone balustrade from passers by on the street. The result is curiously intimate, and very popular with the staff who work there.

But it is in the handling of the conference hall that we see real finesse. This is a large space and it is sharply defined by its architecture, a 1900 version of the Ionic order. Rick Mather Architects have maintained this order, reconstituting it meticulously at one end where they have added a mezzanine floor. The new structure responds to the order: a couple of Modern cylindrical columns stand behind the Ionic columns (I have always thought of these as today's equivalents of the Ionic order), but the result is quiet and completely acceptable. Out of sight from the hall, this enclosed mezzanine provides space for a new print room, entirely Modern in its handling, but with a sympathetic use of timber. Overhead in the hall where there was already a glazed roof, there is now a completely new structure, which follows the old in its general lines. At the open end, where the hall gives on to Elverton Street, there is a series of lattice columns to the *piano nobile* whose outer edges curve gently out towards the base, so that it looks Modern in an entirely 1900ish way.

New, simplified and distinct entrances are provided to both the Society's Headquarters and the conference facilities. The Old Hall has been transformed into a modern conference space. Behind the re-glazed facade of Elverton Street new office space was inserted within the vaulted trusses, above the entrance lobby and mezzanine cafe. These offices extend over two floors behind an internal glazed screen that provides both an acoustic and a visual barrier to the hall but allows natural daylight in. The top floor space vacated by the library and other existing rooms was carefully refurbished without destroying the original fabric of the building.

left: The refurbished main hall, showing the rebuilt office insertion, with a glass wall that allows daylight in and views to the sky, but blocks views down to the hall.
opposite: Plans: ground floor; basement. Sections: short section; long section. The red line indicates the original ground level and extent of the new excavation.

above: Early sketch of Lindley Library showing basement reading room from above, and new ramped access for the disabled, with workstations below.
below: Basement reading room as built. The roof light, as well as providing natural light, gives views of the trees in Vincent Square across the street.
opposite: The new Lindley Library stair links reading rooms and archive facilities.

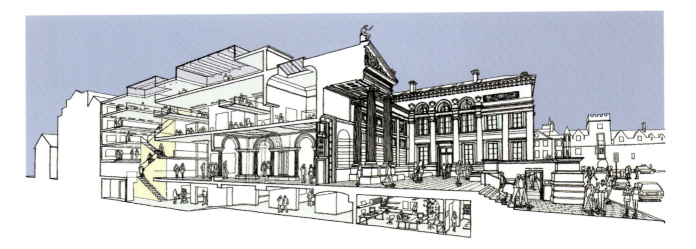

72 At the Ashmolean Museum there was no case for making a new eye-catching volume, but a wish for more galleries that would expand the exhibition space available. Rick Mather Architects have, by careful planning, found room for half a dozen such galleries, dovetailed into the ground floor behind the main frontage, and in all providing 100 per cent more display space, but also an education centre, conservation studios, teaching rooms and study galleries.

Ashmolean Museum Oxford

The Ashmolean Museum, established in 1683, is the oldest museum in Britain. The new building is attached to the rear of the Greek Revival building by Charles Robert Cockerell, built in 1845 as The University Galleries. The Ashmolean Museum relocated to the extended University Galleries in 1894, in 1908 combined to become The Ashmolean Museum of Art and Archaeology, under the keepership of the renowned archaeologist Sir Arthur Evans.

Its collections are among the most varied and extensive in the country, including the most important collection of pre-Dynastic Egyptian material outside Cairo, the most important collection of Raphael drawings in the world and the greatest Anglo-Saxon collections outside the British Museum.

The scheme involves the removal of the existing Victorian buildings behind the Cockerell building, and later piecemeal accretions. These combined to give a very confusing route for the museum visitor.

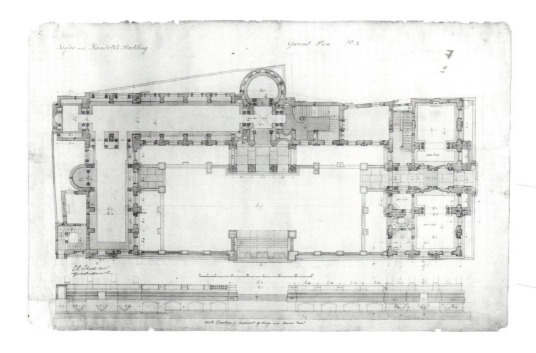

Ashmolean Museum.
left: Original contract drawing, c. 1842.
opposite: Ground floor plan.

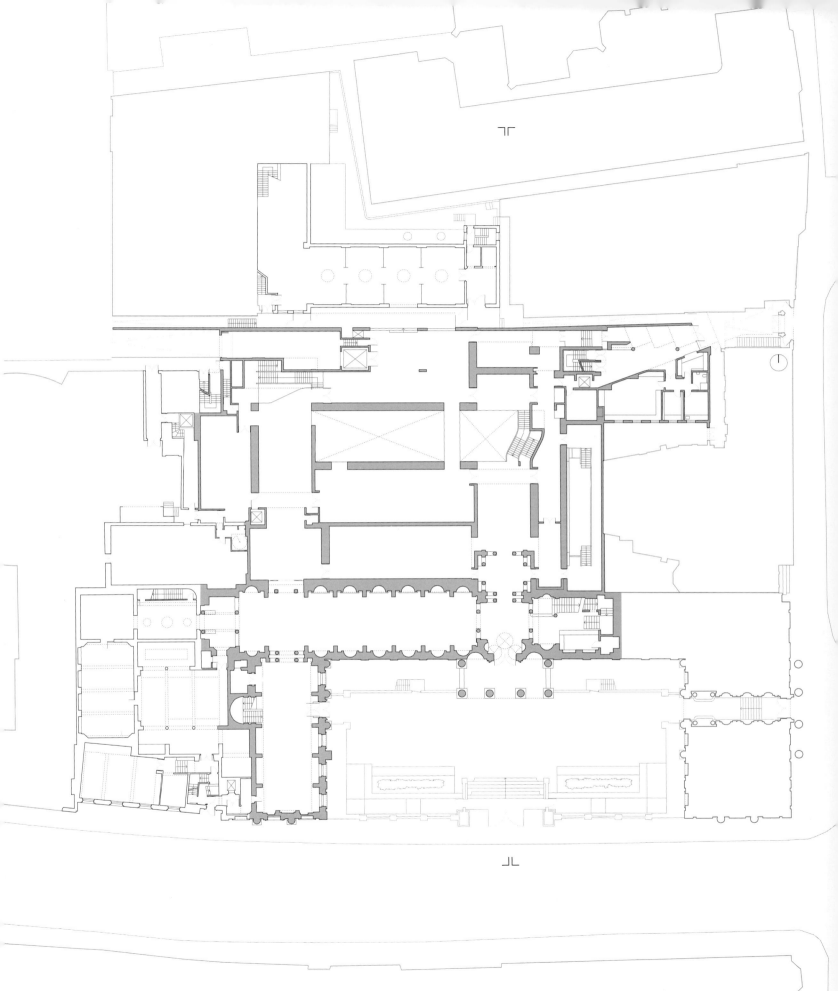

The new building has six storeys, with a floor area of 9,000 sqm (97,000 sqft). The new museum space is built to modern standards, using an environmentally aware and efficient servicing strategy. The building is organised by two major axes established by Cockerell, creating a clear route throughout the building and unifying the entire museum and collection in a coherent manner.

Two staircase lightwells are naturally lit with large windows and roof lights. Natural light is filtered vertically through the building to the lower ground level via inter-connecting, double-height galleries. A new rooftop cafe terrace gives views over the 'dreaming spires' of Oxford.

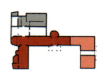
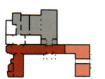
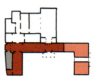

1845   1886   1890   1894   1908

above right: 'Hellfire Plan', 1910. This drawing was commissioned by Sir Arthur Evans to show the risk to the Museum from adjacent properties.
above left: Perspective drawing by CR Cockerell, c. 1845 (V&A Museum).
left and right: The historical development of the Ashmolean Museum has been piecemeal. The diagrams show the slow growth north over time, as space, funds and land became available. The resultant arrangement was labyrinthine and confusing.
opposite: Sections through the portico, looking east (above) and west (below).

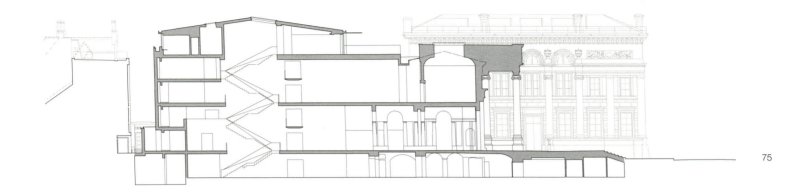

75

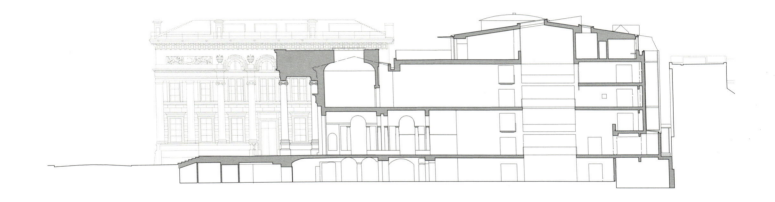

1930's   1944   1955   1960   1990s   2000   2008

above: Model photo showing north-eastern cascading staircase.
below: Aerial photograph montage with the new building from the north-east.
opposite: Lower ground floor plan.

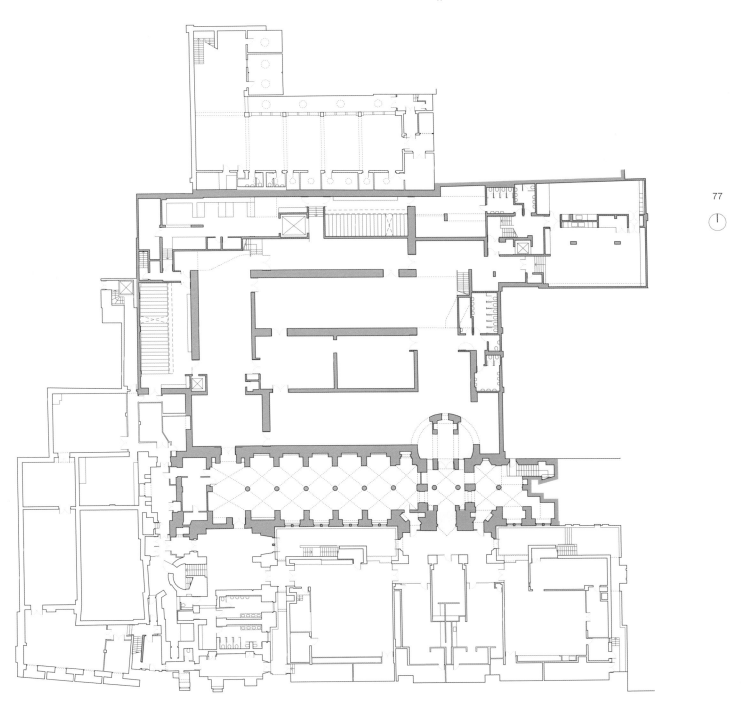

77

Dulwich Picture Gallery

The original Soane building is famous as probably the world's first purpose-built art gallery. It is well known for its series of *enfilade* galleries with roof lanterns, which diffuse natural daylight, creating an even wash of light over the walls—ideal for viewing paintings. The gallery was bombed during the Second World War and rebuilt in the subsequent period of austerity. It was badly in need of refurbishment, and the client held an invited architectural competition in late 1995.

The brief called for all the facilities that a modern gallery requires: to provide a suitable environment for the collection; the housing of a temporary gallery; to improve the visitor support facilities by providing a cafe, toilets, lecture hall and education space; and to improve the back of house facilities, including workshops and a picture store.

Dulwich Picture Gallery.
opposite: The roof and cupola were completely rebuilt. Blackout, solar control, double glazing, improved security and modern lighting are now incorporated, and a new oak floor installed.
above left: Construction painting by C Tyrell, 1812, a research source for the renovation.
above right: The gallery was badly damaged in the Second World War.

But there is no doubt that the most popular of Rick Mather Architects' extensions and interventions to an existing building is their work at the Dulwich Picture Gallery, itself the first example of a type that was to become established in the course of the twentieth century. Here they have done a lot to improve the existing galleries, using both natural and artificial lighting and the application of colour, but so discreetly that it is hard to see their hand. They have provided new accommodation, comprising a new gallery, lecture room, education centre and a restaurant, all linked together by a cloister, in two sections at right angles, out in front of Soane. It thus begins to enclose a sort of forecourt to the main gallery. It is an entirely modest building, beautifully executed. The steel structure is amplified by ladder-like additions in bronze on the outside, which help to screen the large glass windows and increase the sense of enclosure within. Occasional strips of glass in the roof of the cloister lighten the effect, and quietly increase the sense of Modernity. These are developed from the positions of the buttresses in the original chapel, at first corresponding to their whole width, and in the floor two narrower lighting slots mark the edges. The whole comes together into an interior that reflects its situation with the original building. The restaurant has become a well-known rendezvous, not only an amenity for the gallery, but a destination in itself.

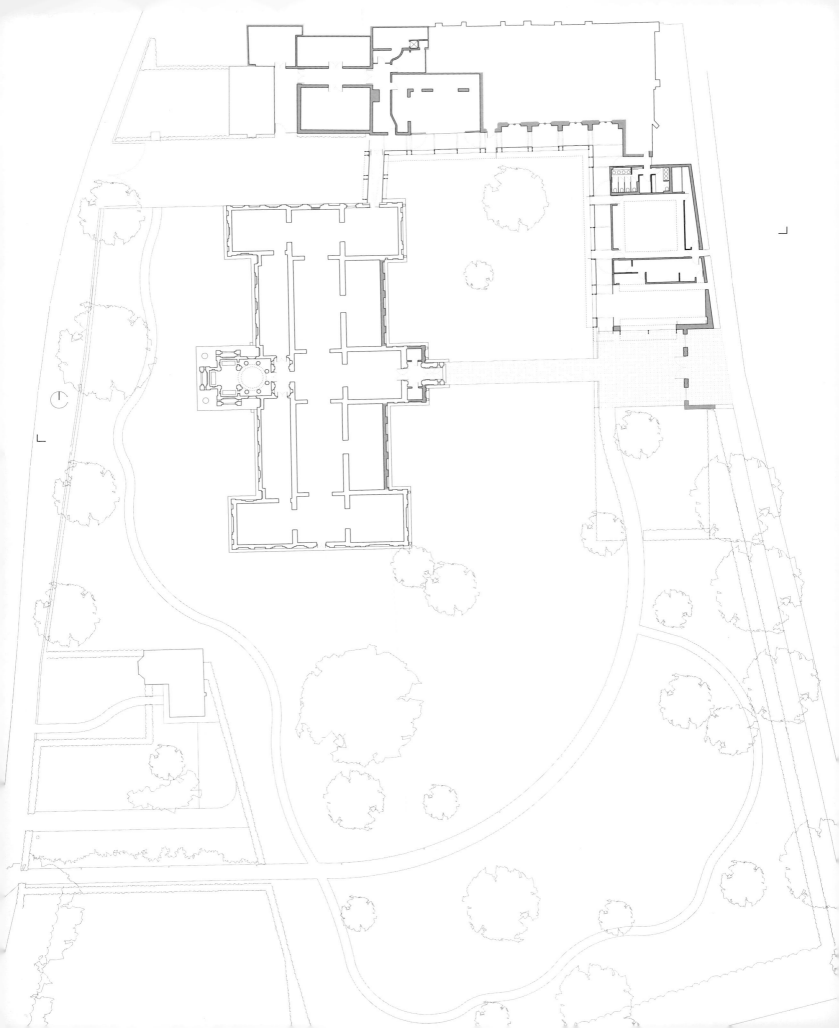

Although there is little visual evidence of change, the original gallery building has been entirely refurbished with computer-controlled variable daylighting through the roof lights, new lighting replacing the previous fluorescent and concealed blackout blinds bringing the picture lighting control within modern conservation standards.

Externally the east facade has been remodelled by replacing the redundant 1950s windows with a series of blind arches, echoing the original, and creating greater internal hanging space. The gardens have been subtly remodelled with a new footpath leading to the gallery entrance, creating a promenade within the newly opened up south garden.

It is clear that part of its appeal is its location in relation to the art gallery. You feel that you are at the gallery while having lunch. It seems that Rick Mather Architects are not only experts on the small details that create a sense of being in a special place, but that they have a sense also of the power and presence of a building in its original form. They clearly appreciated the Dulwich Gallery. This is something that James Stirling also had, and it may be the most important part of an architectural talent: the sheer enjoyment of architectural quality, wherever it is found. It raises the possibility of seeing buildings as special objects, embodying qualities that we recognise and would not wish to be without. It also makes us aware of the space outside of them that the buildings influence by their character, and hence of the space between buildings. This is important when the buildings are lined up to form a street, which doesn't happen today so much as it did. It is also important when the buildings are arranged to occupy an expansive space, like a university campus. This is why a talent for placing buildings together may be such an enormous part of what an architect has to do.

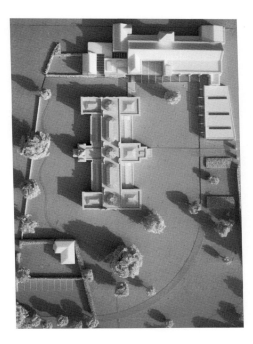

opposite: The picture store, workshop and education room are to the north and the gallery/lecture room and cafe are to the east of the original building.
above: Section through the original gallery with the new cloister and chapel in the background.
right: Design development model, leaving the gallery freestanding and new facilities at the perimeter, along the street, connected by the glass cloister.

The new building suggests a formal quadrangle creating a cloistered entrance garden in front of the gallery. Central to the design is the cloister, which links the cafe, temporary gallery and education space to the main picture gallery. It mediates between the main gallery and the new building, taking its rhythm of bronze structure and glass roof lights from the buttresses of the adjacent chapel.

The new building is designed as a thick garden wall and consequently uses the red brick of the wall with glass inserts to distinguish the individual elements. The southern facade of the cafe and the facades of the cloister all slide open to engage the main gallery and the garden. The glazing is shaded by the stainless steel mesh hung between supports acting as a *brise-soleil*. The temporary exhibition gallery can also be adapted to become a lecture room by lowering the floor. The new education space is inserted between the existing chapel and the back of house facilities.

The new cloister frames the existing gallery and creates a new quadrangle as Soane originally intended. The windows slide open to full width. The gallery facade was rebuilt to more closely follow Soane's original design.

We have seen something of this already: at Keble, everyone expected Rick Mather Architects to put the first building on the site: there was clearly room for it. By placing it to one side, on the edge, they showed a sense of the space outside of the building. Instead of becoming a marginal strip, it became a positive well-defined space, leaving plenty of room for another building, a building that also pulled back from the site to follow another edge, so that the two together made a quadrangle with the existing buildings, adding a typical university feature that helps to make the novelty acceptable. It wasn't so different from the result at the Maritime Museum, where we end up with an entirely new space in the old quadrangle. It is this sense of the value of space, whether inside or outside the building, that illustrates what the work of an architect should be.

above: The new wing links to the adjacent village with a temporary exhibition gallery (lit by a frameless glass skylight) and cafe.
left: Competition drawing of the new cloister.
opposite: The northern end of Soane's original *enfilade* of galleries.

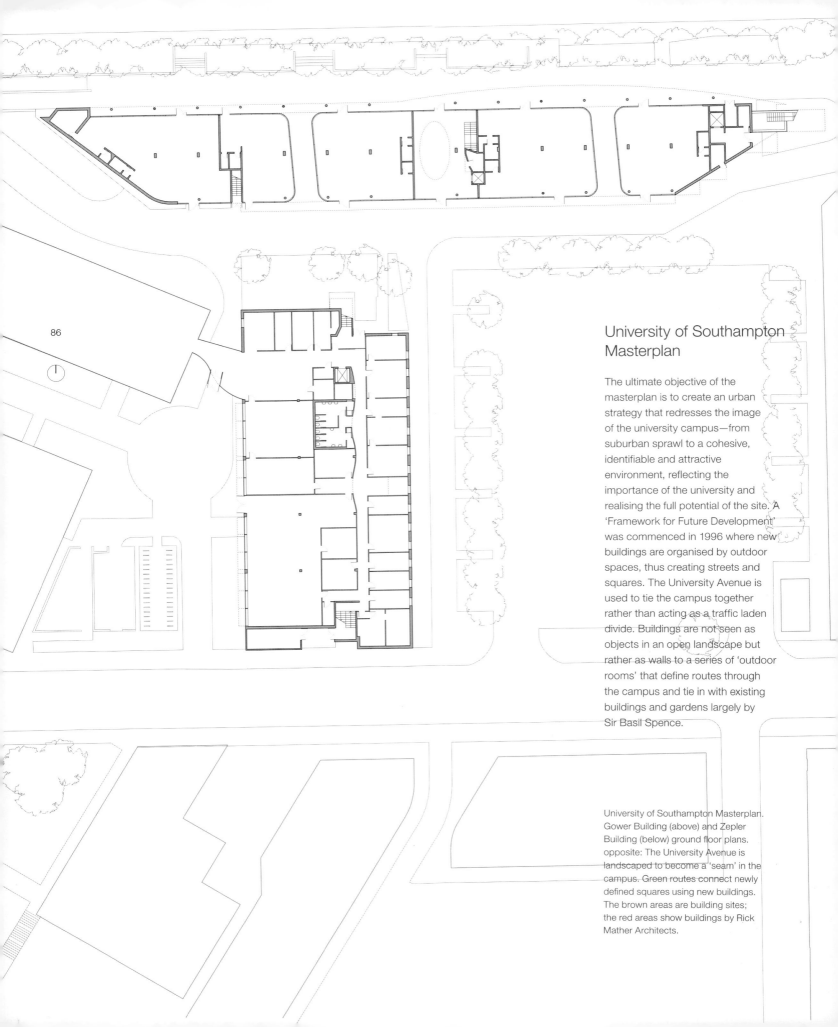

University of Southampton Masterplan

The ultimate objective of the masterplan is to create an urban strategy that redresses the image of the university campus—from suburban sprawl to a cohesive, identifiable and attractive environment, reflecting the importance of the university and realising the full potential of the site. A 'Framework for Future Development' was commenced in 1996 where new buildings are organised by outdoor spaces, thus creating streets and squares. The University Avenue is used to tie the campus together rather than acting as a traffic laden divide. Buildings are not seen as objects in an open landscape but rather as walls to a series of 'outdoor rooms' that define routes through the campus and tie in with existing buildings and gardens largely by Sir Basil Spence.

University of Southampton Masterplan. Gower Building (above) and Zepler Building (below) ground floor plans. opposite: The University Avenue is landscaped to become a 'seam' in the campus. Green routes connect newly defined squares using new buildings. The brown areas are building sites; the red areas show buildings by Rick Mather Architects.

With this skill in envisaging how buildings can work together, we are now in a position to propose a strategy, what in the parlance is known as a 'masterplan'.

This kind of work began around 1988 when Rick Mather Architects had already completed some buildings for the University of East Anglia, including the Climatic Research Unit, 1985. Later, in 1993, came Constable Terrace, a block of student accommodation. The first is a small cylindrical block, the second a long undulating curve. They both appear unusual in a context hitherto confined to squarish buildings, and they both contribute towards the overall shape of a largely rural campus, made famous first by Denys Lasdun, with his serrated residences, and then Norman Foster, with the Sainsbury Centre. By the time Rick Mather Architects were asked to design a further building they had been accepted as the masterplanner for the campus as a whole, providing a grand strategy in the form of a 25 year development plan.

88

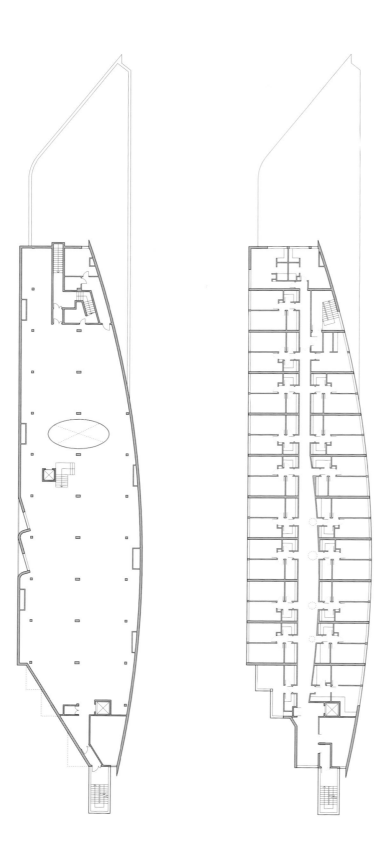

The Zepler Building extends from the Faculty of Electronics and was the first academic building to be built under the masterplan. The Gower Building was the second. It houses shops and banks, bringing life and activity to the edge of the campus. The building creates a new landmark at the entrance to the campus, announcing the university's presence.

The Sports Complex is situated on a prime site in the centre of the campus. The organisation of the building functions are arranged to animate the University Avenue, with a full view of the new swimming pool and cafe entrance through the full-height glazing. The fitness suite tiered above the double-height reception and cafe is also visible to passing pedestrians.

Gower Building.
left: Plans: second floor residential accommodation; first floor bookshop.
opposite: The new building acts as a signpost at the entrance to the campus.

A similar pattern emerges with the University of Southampton, where Rick Mather Architects were first asked to provide two buildings on infill sites: the Gower Building and the Zepler Building, and later the sports centre completed in 2004. The masterplan for the whole campus transforms it from suburban sprawl to a cohesive and attractive total environment, realising the full potential of the land.

The Jubilee Sports Complex has all the facilities of a sports centre: a six lane, 25 metre swimming pool, an eight court badminton hall, and a large fitness centre. There is spectator seating sufficient for hosting national and international competitions, along with a large reception area and cafe. So it has proved very popular with the public, and has even raised the level of architecture as a subject of conversation. To fit the site, one side of the building is elegantly curved, which fact alone takes it out of routine consideration.

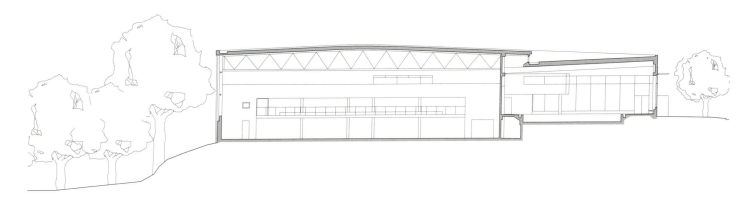

The site falls away to the west from University Avenue to the University Botanical Gardens. The building design utilises this natural site condition by locating the large sports hall one level below the street, reducing its apparent bulk from the botanical garden below.

The Sports Complex includes a swimming pool, a competition size hall for basketball and eight badminton courts, and a fitness centre, as well as a large reception area, a cafe and staff offices.

Sports Complex
above: Section.
middle: Inverted seam metal cladding acts as a backdrop to the trees above the botanical gardens.
left: Activity in the pool is indirectly lit from a clerestory on the left. The cafe and fitness centre above overlooks the pool.
opposite: Street level plan.

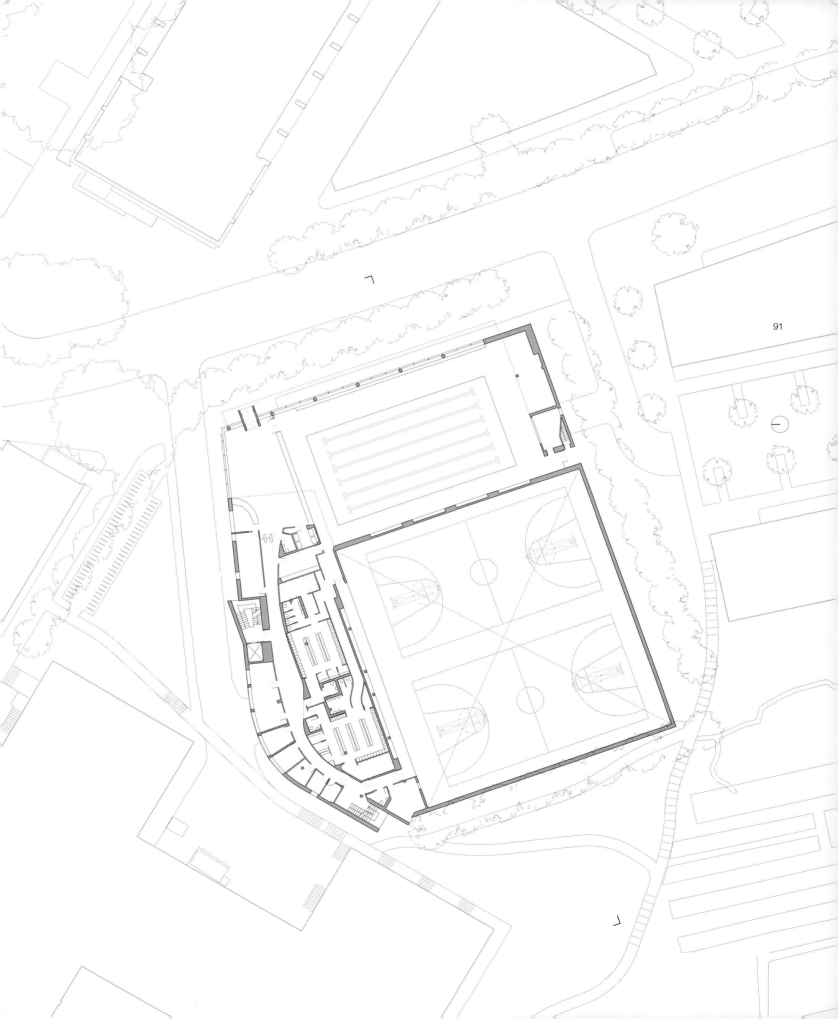

91

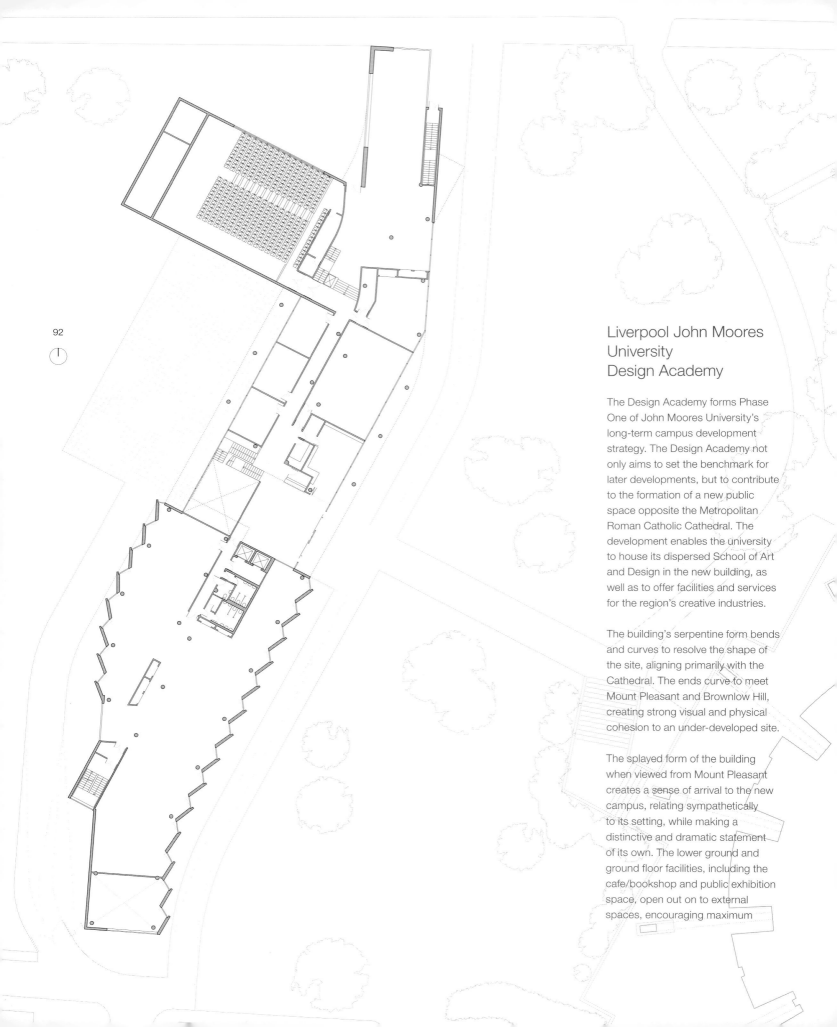

Liverpool John Moores University Design Academy

The Design Academy forms Phase One of John Moores University's long-term campus development strategy. The Design Academy not only aims to set the benchmark for later developments, but to contribute to the formation of a new public space opposite the Metropolitan Roman Catholic Cathedral. The development enables the university to house its dispersed School of Art and Design in the new building, as well as to offer facilities and services for the region's creative industries.

The building's serpentine form bends and curves to resolve the shape of the site, aligning primarily with the Cathedral. The ends curve to meet Mount Pleasant and Brownlow Hill, creating strong visual and physical cohesion to an under-developed site.

The splayed form of the building when viewed from Mount Pleasant creates a sense of arrival to the new campus, relating sympathetically to its setting, while making a distinctive and dramatic statement of its own. The lower ground and ground floor facilities, including the cafe/bookshop and public exhibition space, open out on to external spaces, encouraging maximum

Liverpool John Moores University Design Academy.
opposite: Ground floor plan. Studio windows angle out to catch north light and exclude low east and west sun.
above: View from the Cathedral podium.

One of the most interesting results of the masterplan approach is emerging in the proposals for Liverpool John Moores University. It is a prodigious site near the Catholic Cathedral, and it will certainly give a new face to an institution that has hitherto existed in a piecemeal fashion. The first building is the Design Academy, a building of unusual shape, long and gently double curved, with uniform elevations to measure up to the scale of the Cathedral. The presentation drawings for this project are superb, with a suitably scaled photograph of the Cathedral in the background, and their excellence gives a hint of how Mather gets on with his clients: he puts out a major effort for each one.

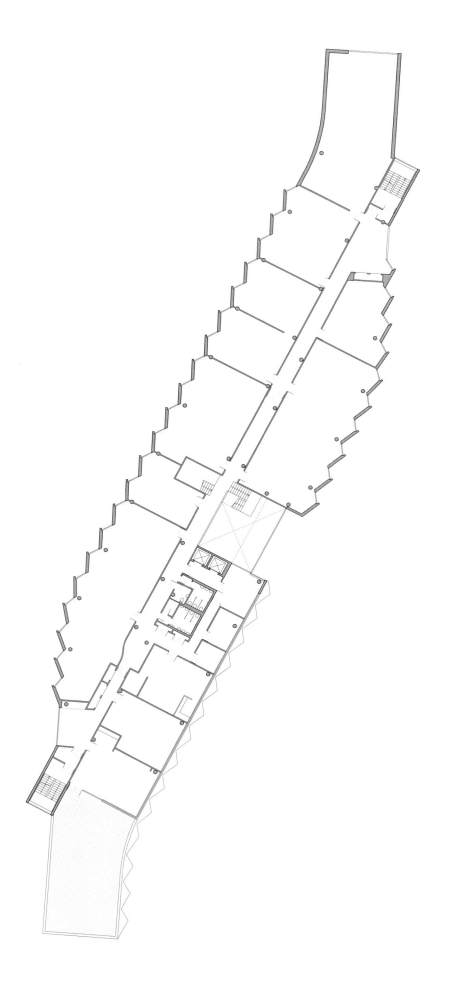

activity outside as well as inside the building. The upper storeys are set back to create tiered roof terraces which afford views across the city.

The main entrance aligns with the west axis of the Cathedral. This space connects upper and lower ground levels with views of the Cathedral. Unified by a dramatic staircase, with informal spill out space and views into each level, this is the social heart of the building, facilitating interaction between the different departments and public facilities. The lower ground and ground floors showcase the Academy's creative talent, through the public galleries, exhibition, multi-purpose spaces, project room and studios.

left: Second floor plan.
opposite above: West elevation, with Cathedral behind.
opposite below: The atrium frames the Cathedral through high spaces around the stair.

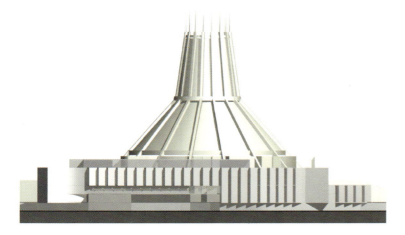

The studios and teaching spaces, located on the ground and upper floors, are designed to be as flexible as possible, maximising light, space and energy efficiency for the benefit of the students and staff. The largest body of studios are located on the east and west where they find their expression in the form of splayed windows, which admit controlled north light and shade east and west light. The academic offices are articulated by continuous strip windows.

The building's profile with its stepped roof terraces responds to views from the Cathedral; the top floor is recessed from the perimeter and set back from the north and south ends to form roof terraces and reduce the apparent mass of the building.

Coking Works Masterplan Chesterfield

This 98 hectare (242 acre) site is amongst the most contaminated in western Europe, following decades of mining activity and lime, iron and coke production. It is being managed by East Midlands Development Agency, and funded through English Partnerships National Coalfield Programme.

This project is literally planning from the ground up. The level of toxicity of the soil requires that the entire site be excavated to a depth of several metres and treated on site, sterilising it and doubling its volume. The opportunity thus presents itself to generate a new landscape. The fundamental design decision was that the new topography would be neither spuriously naturalistic, nor rigorously geometric.

Another project that is in its early days is the Coking Works Masterplan for Chesterfield. This will transform an industrial waste land, much of it contaminated, into healthy landscape, or rather townscape, providing sites for new institutional buildings for the city of Chesterfield. This project will follow the whole trajectory for reclamation, transforming wasteland into public amenity.

Coking Works Masterplan Chesterfield.
above: Over a period of seven years the existing contaminated former coking works is to be transformed into a new landscape topography, following the treatment of the soil.
opposite: The new landscape with buildings.

The tradition of Capability Brown and William Kent presented itself as an obvious precedent for the large-scale remaking of the landscape, with the fundamental difference that it would no longer be carried out by manual labour in the service of privileged whimsy. The form was generated using computer modelling in response to the surrounding landscape, the historical manipulation of the site, sustainable drainage strategies and the potential future urbanisation of the site. The idea was that the landscape should appear as if it had once been a settlement but had returned to a state of nature, the aim being to ensure that the place should appear complete whether or not the potential residential and commercial development of the site were to materialise.

Of course, the time scale has been stretched out, but the first phase of Rick Mather Architects' masterplan for the South Bank Centre—the area around the Royal Festival Hall, National Theatre and London Eye—is near completion. In 1999, they were chosen from over 70 international candidates, and the proposals adopted the following year. The masterplan is now being implemented, and even with partial occupation is already transforming the area.

The design includes a new urban street setting for Belvedere Road, and the park that stretches from it to the river. In an area that has long been inhibited by high level concrete walkways, relics of a time when London was to be recast as a two level city, the aim is to regenerate the use of the ground level, and to encourage greater activity, diversity and accessibility for the site as a whole. Entrances are brought down to ground level, all frontages are made active, and servicing routes are taken out of the public realm. Additional open space is created, including two new urban squares, one of which is nearly complete. With entrances, cafes and foyers at street level, the Hayward Gallery, Queen Elizabeth Hall and Purcell Room are all to be substantially expanded in line with their international status, making use of the ground level that has previously been appropriated by skateboarders. This change has already benefited the Royal Festival Hall, which is being independently renovated. As proposed in the masterplan the ground level river frontage is now lined with busy new restaurants and a new building shields the Festival Hall from the Hungerford Bridge.

A massive expansion of available space is made possible because the proposal envisages tilting up a portion of the park, thus treating Jubilee Gardens partly as a roof garden, tilted towards the river view, in order to create new volume underneath it. This is perfectly practicable, if rather radical for an official client to accept, but the landscape design selected has made use of this idea.

South Bank Centre Masterplan, London

London's South Bank Centre (SBC) is the largest arts complex in the world. The site is approximately 12 hectares (30 acres), bounded by the River Thames to the north-west, Waterloo Bridge to the north-east, Belvedere Road to the south-east, and the London Eye to the south-west.

The masterplan provides a framework for the improvement and extension of existing cultural facilities and public realm at this important central London site, including the Royal Festival Hall, the Hayward Gallery, the Queen Elizabeth Hall, the Purcell Room, and the British Film Institute (comprising the National Film Theatre, the Museum of the Moving Image and the BFI library). After continuing development and refinement of the masterplan, many of the proposals have been agreed or implemented with Phase One currently underway.

above: The new restaurants on the riverfront of Festival Hall.
opposite: South Bank Centre Masterplan.

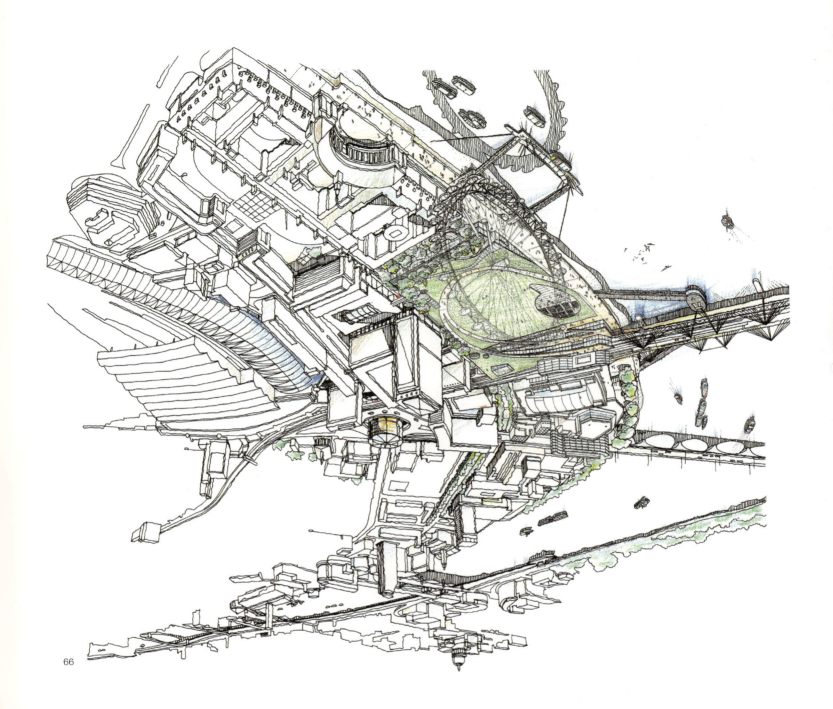

A series of principles were established as a first step, forming the South Bank Urban Design Strategy: improving accessibility, legibility and the public realm—there are currently major conflicts between pedestrian movement and vehicular servicing traffic, isolating the cultural institutions and creating general confusion for visitors. Entrances to all destinations are located at ground level; the arts venues currently have much of their main access from indirect high-level routes with dark, dead space beneath. A greater mix of use aimed at bringing a richer blend of visitors to the site over longer periods of the day. All building frontages throughout the site are activated with foyers, cafes and arts-related retail. Linkages are improved between public open space, cultural facilities, public transport, highway

The South Bank Centre.
above: Festival of Britain, 1951. The Royal Festival Hall is the centre of the arts complex and is the only remaining element of the Festival.
below: The South Bank Centre is in the heart of London. Facing across the Thames, from left, Westminster, the West End, Covent Garden and the City.
opposite above: The existing service routes (left) were rearranged (centre) enabling the creation of two new public spaces.
opposite: The masterplan proposes active frontage along Belvedere Road and a gateway to Jubilee Gardens.

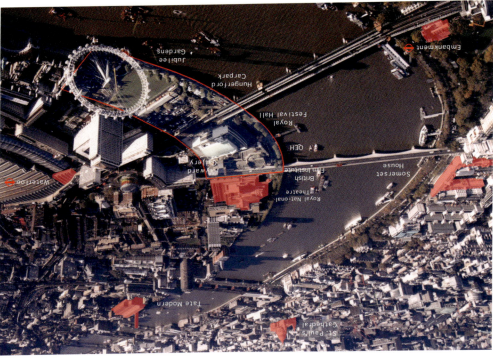

The first phase, concentrated on the site defined by the Royal Festival Hall (RFH), the Hayward Gallery, the Queen Elizabeth Hall and the Purcell Room, creates three new major public spaces—'Festival Square' to the Belvedere Road side of the RFH, 'Riverside Landscape' to the Thames side of the RFH and 'River Link Square' that connects the two, developed in detail by Gross.Max. Landscape Architects. A new 'liner' building alongside the Hungerford Railway Bridge to the south of the RFH defines a grand new route up to the Golden Jubilee Hungerford Pedestrian Bridges and shields the public and the RFH from the high-level railway. The building conceals existing service routes and decants existing office space from the RFH, allowing it to turn more space over to public use. Additional arts-related commercial space is interspersed at peripheral positions at all levels to increase the mix of use and activity. New cafes are incorporated on street and river frontages of the RFH. Service routes are removed from the public realm and are discreetly relocated behind major building blocks, releasing significant areas of public space while linking and reinforcing key destinations.

above: Section through the new Jubilee Gardens.

opposite: The Hayward Gallery is brought down to ground with active frontage addressing the new 'Festival Square'.

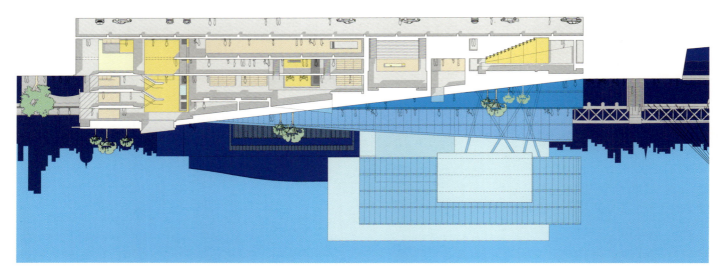

networks, and other key destinations looking beyond the limits of the South Bank Centre site.

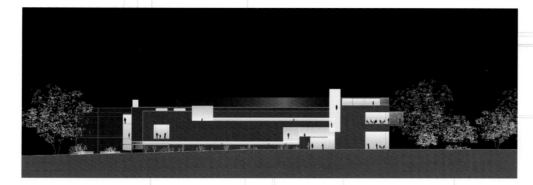

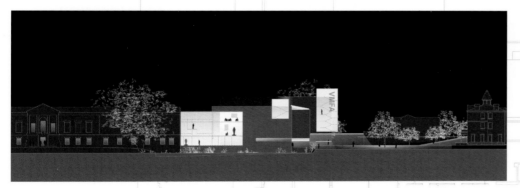

The work for the Virginia Museum of Fine Arts in Richmond, funded by both the state and private donors, includes the masterplan for the whole campus. Part of the new proposals complete and regularise the existing building, but the greater part comes together in a new entrance wing which will house new galleries for both permanent and temporary exhibitions, a library, cafe, restaurant and offices. The new wing will be linked to the existing building across an atrium, which becomes the new central space. Light floods down from above. Across the space are six thin glass sided bridges connecting the upper levels in both buildings. This space is dramatised by the way in which the walls of the new portion have been made to undulate, in two sections one above the other, in a broken rhythm creating a counterpoint. With glass floors and ceilings to the projecting volumes thus created local interest will be raised, while the building as a whole becomes more stimulating. Where the new building faces the boulevard there will be a 12 metre (40 foot) high window displaying pieces from the collection. From inside there will be views eastward towards downtown, conversely giving the museum, for the first time, an open presence in the city. The governing idea here was to turn the museum back towards the street, and look towards the city. It illustrates how Rick Mather Architects can manipulate internal volumes in such a way as to provide a bonus in the way the building fits into the city plan.

Virginia Museum of Fine Arts

Rick Mather Architects were selected from an international field of competitors in 2001 to masterplan and design a major expansion and renovation of this highly reputed, 65 year old encyclopaedic museum and its 5.5 hectare (13.5 acre) campus. This marks the office's first major commission in the United States.

The expansion plan envisages adding more than 9,300 sqm (100,000 sqft) to the existing 22,300 sqm (240,000 sqft) building. Upon completion, the new museum complex will include a 1.6 hectare (4 acre) Sculpture Garden, extensive new galleries, educational facilities, visitor service areas, administrative offices and a parking deck.

The approach opens the main VMFA building up to the city and provides extensive new space for the museum's art collections. The new five level glass and limestone entrance wing features two floors of permanent collection galleries.

Virginia Museum of Fine Arts.
above left: The north elevation to the entrance court and the east elevation to the Boulevard and city.
opposite: Ground floor plan.

105

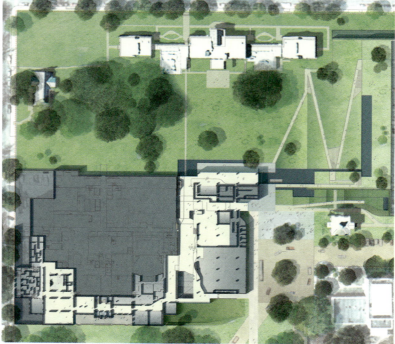

A dedicated temporary exhibitions gallery level is capable of housing major international travelling shows. In addition, the new wing holds a library, gift shop, conservation facilities, a 150 seat lecture hall, offices, and a cafe and restaurant overlooking the Sculpture Garden. The new wing is linked to the existing building by glass bridges across the central atrium space, acting as a main street that connects new

above: Sectional model through the atrium.
left: The entire masterplan encompasses a new Sculpture Garden extending up over the parking deck, a major new extension building and alterations to the existing building.
opposite above: Section through the entrance space with galleries, offices and conservation studios above.
opposite below: Section through the atrium and new galleries.

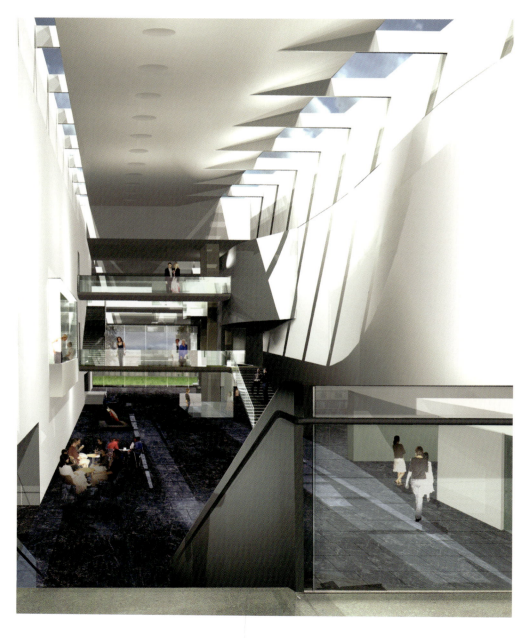

and existing over three levels. Work to the existing building includes a new education centre, and the reconfiguration of existing galleries.

The VMFA's purpose is announced to the city by a high window facing the Boulevard, displaying pieces from the museum's collection. From inside there are views towards downtown, which is visible for the first time from the museum site. The new Entrance Plaza acts as a square onto the main street, bringing the public to the new Sculpture Garden and completing the vision of this campus masterplan.

opposite: The atrium culminates in a 12 metre (40 foot) picture window facing the city. 'Smart' glass allows the signage to change on the glass to the right.

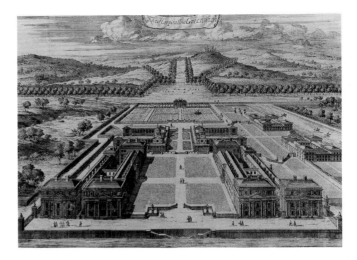

Rick Mather Architects' work in the National Maritime Museum is backed up by a strategic masterplan which they have prepared for buildings and landscape: there may not be much left to build anew at Greenwich, but since it has been designated as a World Heritage Site, it is clearly a sensitive object, and has to be well looked after. There may be some amelioration of the interiors, but most of it will consist of attention to the landscape as an important aspect of the River Thames. Rick Mather Architects have also been selected to develop a masterplan for the Natural History Museum in South Kensington. Their plan identifies sites for new buildings to allow the museum to be able to display more of its vast collection. It will also look at how to improve visitor circulation. They have also provided a strategic masterplan for Stowe School, which begins with two new girls' boarding houses. All these sites are of national importance, and if Mather is in the running, it's not because he has friends in Parliament, it's because he has won competitions. He has an American attitude of having a go, and the work he has put out has met with a response.

In all these endeavours there is a constant give and take between the aim to provide a conscientious report that will help the client in managing the land, and the more or less constant desire of an architect to make sites for his own buildings. But there is also a fundamental desire, which no architect is without, to expand into the built environment, to take in the outward momentum that a building exerts on its surroundings, to end up with a piece of designed total environment. I don't think a single architect is capable of designing a whole city: a city by definition must be heterogeneous, a mixed bag. But it is fascinating to explore how far can one go, outward, before one's limitations become obvious.

Greenwich Landscape Masterplan

This strategic and detailed masterplan was developed with a number of client bodies for both the National Maritime Museum, including the Queen's House, and the Old Royal Naval College either side of Romney Road within the newly designated World Heritage Site, Maritime Greenwich. As well as the landscape masterplan the work also included the new Neptune Court at the National Maritime Museum and works to the Pepys Building to make it the Greenwich Visitor Orientation Centre. The strategy ensures that the unique character of the site is enhanced by coordination of routes, landscaping and buildings.

Greenwich Landscape Masterplan.
above: *The Hospital at Greenwich*, Johannes Kip, c. 1710.
opposite: The existing Greenwich World Heritage Site.

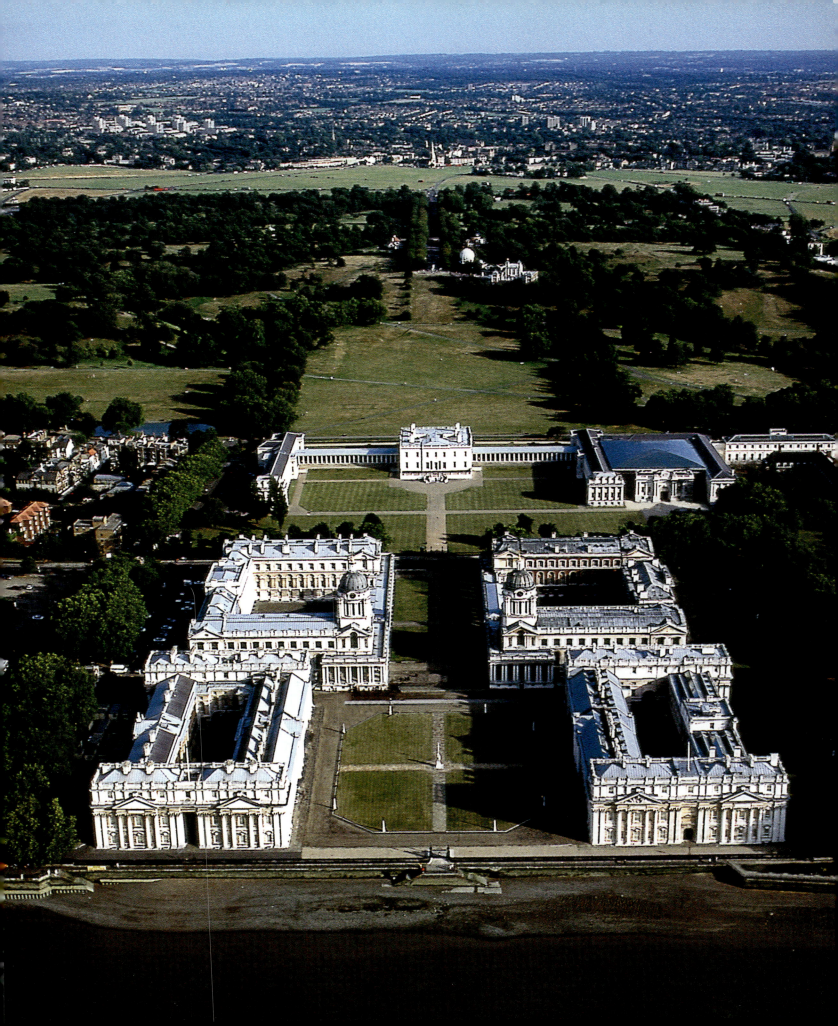

112

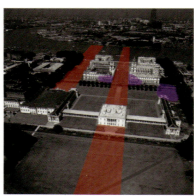

The development consolidates various approaches with regard to the restoration and management of the landscape, unifying its key elements and clarifying the relationship of landscape and buildings in an appropriate manner based on historical analysis. This entails creating a landscape management framework, including a tree management plan and parking and vehicular access strategies to improve links, both physical and visual, reuniting the site with the Royal Park, the River Thames and its urban setting.

above: The Pepys Building.
left: The landscape masterplan for the National Maritime Museum and the Old Royal Naval College seeks to reinvigorate their reciprocal relationship by carefully managing tree planting and controlling views between the two and, most important, visually linking the Maritime Museum with the River Thames.
opposite: The Greenwich Landscape Masterplan.

Constable Terrace,
University of East Anglia, Norwich.

The situation that developed at the University of East Anglia is crucial here. The story begins in 1984 with a commission for a modest addendum—a building for the School of Information Studies, a wing linked at one end to Denys Lasdun's main 'teaching wall'. It helped, no doubt, that Rick Mather Architects were recommended to the university by the then consultant architect, Norman Foster (who liked the Peter Eaton Antiquarian Bookshop and Architectural Association renovation). Gradually the brief expanded to include a School of Education, so that the single wing turned into a three sided courtyard, with the link to the back of the teaching wall at one corner. The open side of the courtyard is defined by a coppice of trees, birches that were the subject of a research project and therefore untouchable. The windows are grouped in relation to the panels of the wall covering, and expand at the entrances to make them easier to find, and to enliven the massing.

This building was followed the next year with the more modest building for the Climatic Research Unit. This came in as a regular cylinder only three storeys high, of only 13 metres (43 feet) diameter, in the same area near the Lasdun building, and clearly another addendum. The surface of the cylinder is decorated at base and around the top, but there is no cornice, the forms are basic. At the entrance, an L shaped recess exposes a cylindrical column, and the recess thus formed adds to the enjoyment of the cylinder. Both of these buildings are in an easy Modern style, with white tiled walls carried on prefabricated panels, punctuated by groups of windows spaced according to planning exigencies. But their geometry is forthright and crisp. They were the first to be done for a public client, and they must have produced some satisfaction, for by 1988 Rick Mather Architects had been appointed as masterplanner to the university. Evidently, their sensitivity to the external effect of Lasdun's buildings as well as the internal organisation was in play from the beginning.

University of East Anglia Norwich

The 25 year development plan for the expansion of the University of East Anglia, a landmark 1960s campus originally designed by Denys Lasdun, was commissioned in 1988. This plan identified suitable sites for new student residences, to the west of the campus near Norman Foster's Sainsbury Centre and to the east near existing halls of residence. The masterplan allows for individual buildings to be added to the scheme along new streets and pedestrian routes which re-orientate the primary circulation level to the ground.

The double curve of Constable Terrace is a soft reference to Lasdun's 45 degree angles and defines a large outdoor space in front of the Sainsbury Centre. Constable Terrace contains 400 bedrooms. Nelson Court also provides 400 bedrooms arranged around a courtyard opening to the south to the lake and countryside.

University of East Anglia, Norwich. Added to this 1960s megastructure are: Constable Terrace (under construction), Nelson Court (bottom left) and the Drama Studio to its left.

The residential units have ten bedrooms with communal space and kitchen at ground level, forming a large terrace house. This avoids the institutional character of a hall of residence yet is of an appropriate scale for the campus when combined into terraces that define outdoor spaces.

There are also flatlettes on the top floor, accessed from a lift and stairs at the end of each block. The living/dining/kitchen open south to sunny terraces and the adjacent access route. All houses overlook this route, and face south, gaining maximum benefit from the sun.

above left: Early design development sketch.
above right: The ground floor living rooms have terraces which address the main routes and face the sun.
opposite left: Ground floor communal space, with concealed lighting that emphasises the building's form.
opposite right: Constable Terrace's undulating top floor corridor.

Their reputation went up with the next building, known as Constable Terrace, a group of student residences. This is four storeys, and takes the form of a long undulating curved block stretching more or less along an east-west axis. The majority of rooms are broken up into groups of 10 bedroom, three storey 'houses', accessed by a central staircase, each having its own door and sharing a common room and kitchen. Along the top floor are disposed two bedroom flatlets for older students.

At the time when these residences were designed they constituted one of the first as well as the largest low-energy scheme in the UK. The main aim was to retain heat, and this has led to the adoption of a deep plan, with the windows of major spaces facing south to benefit from maximum heat gain in winter. The skin of the building is more or less sealed (with individual windows being allowed to open marginally) and full ventilation is achieved by a mechanical system which recovers heat from the extracted air. The walls above ground floor are white, and the windows are cleverly grouped in pairs on either side of the panel joints. This reduces the scale, since the paired windows tend to read as one unit.

In addition, the top floor flatlets are protected by an overhang which projects as a continuous cornice along the building and accentuates its sinuous line. This originated from the university's insistence that a pitched roof should be employed. The butterfly roof adopted has satisfied this requirement. At the ends, the form of the roof is apparent, although the two halves are treated as separate one way pitches, which has the further effect of breaking up the mass of what is in fact a large building, and avoiding a too institutional scale. This is reinforced by the windows, which vary as

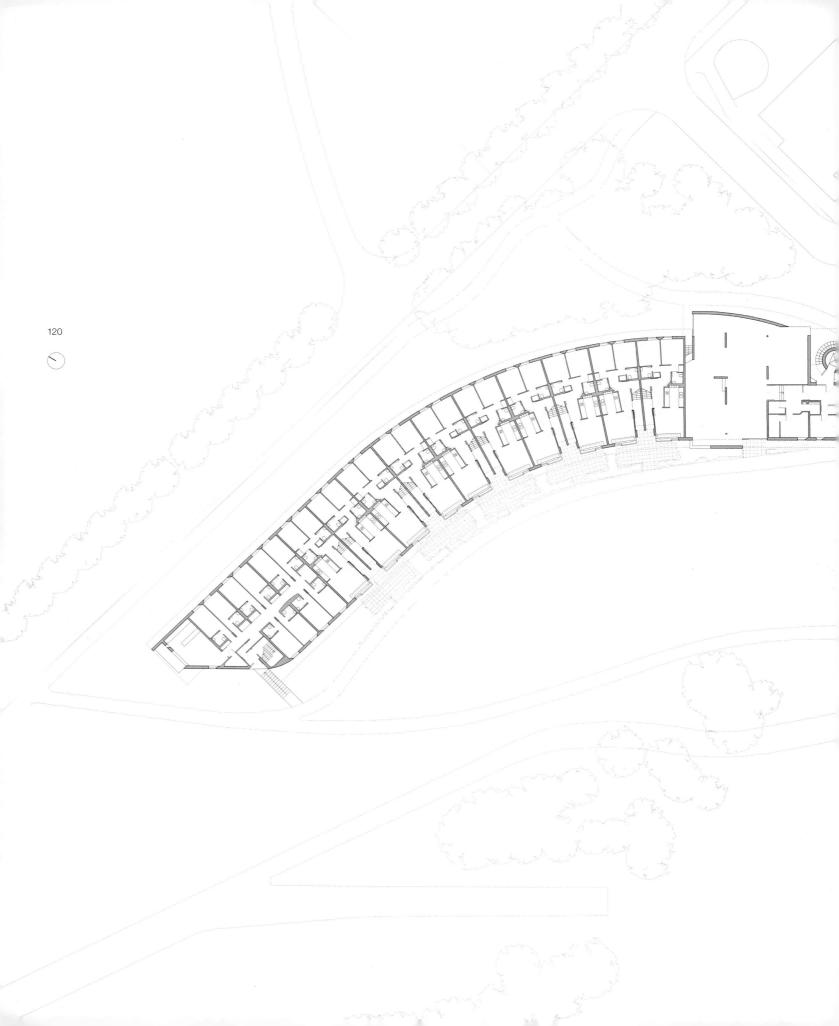

120

Constable Terrace, ground floor plan. The large common room is in the centre, next to the lift and stair to the top floor.

between the rooms below and the flats above. A further break in the regularity is provided by a gap in the building, about halfway along its length. At this point, the roof structure continues unbroken, and the windows again make an interesting pattern. But it is not just visual variety that is followed here: a long building can be boring, it is good to be able to penetrate it and see the other side, without being forced all the way along. And, for me, there is a need to admit that my initial prejudice towards roof overhangs has by now melted away. Without this element, much of the subtlety would have disappeared. It is worth noting that the arguments were more to do with cultural expectations than with sun shading. The building has a carefully thought-out energy plan, but the only sun shades used are to protect the large windows of the students' common rooms on the ground floor. Here they go with the larger aim of persuading the students to sit out in front of their south-facing windows, where they get a view of life as well as sun.

The success of the energy strategy employed here may be gauged from the fact that no central heating is required. A very similar policy and layout was adopted in the construction of Nelson Court, a group of residences placed at the other end of the site, commanding wide views over parkland. The main block has four storeys

The gateway in the centre of Constable Terrace is framed by the circular lift core and spiral stair to the top floor flats. The cables both support the stair treads and railings, and limit access to the stairs.

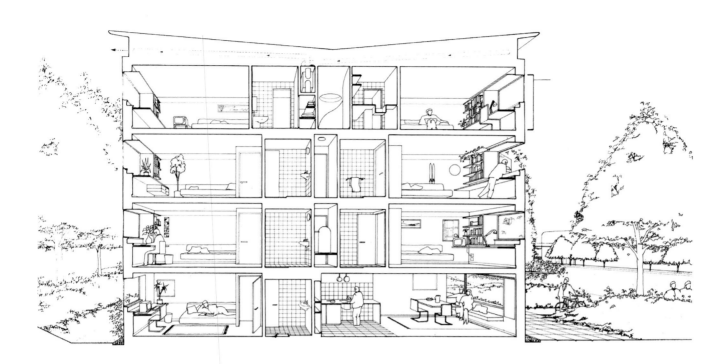

opposite: Uplighting on eaves.
above: Constable Terrace and Nelson Court section. This was the first large-scale low-energy/green engineered scheme in Britain, although Rick Mather Architects had been using these strategies since 1981. High levels of insulation and close fitting double glazed windows mean that virtually no heat is lost through the structure of the building. This, combined with heat transferred from stale air extracted to the fresh air coming in, means no central heating is required—people and equipment provide all the heat needed. Summer cooling is achieved by opening windows.
right: Plans: top floor flats; first and second floor student rooms; ground floor kitchen/living/dining and two bedrooms.

of student rooms, the windows again grouped in pairs. A similar overhanging sun shade—or cornice—defines each leg of the plan, which is divided into straight runs that form between them a couple of courtyards arranged in an S shape. Again, the ends of the blocks, and the breaks between the runs, are given some variety of window treatment which helps to create individuality. Because the roof is thus broken at the corners, the building seems to be made up of small parts, and a gross overall effect is avoided. Yet the two schemes between them provide homes for some 800 students.

The story of East Anglia illustrates how Rick Mather Architects pay attention to all aspects of the architects' problem: planning strategy, site layout, landscape design, individual building massing and detail plans, energy policy and constructional details, the social gain and, of course, the aesthetic effect—all have been considered and all work together in the success of the whole. The story is one of beginning with bit parts and ending up writing the play. The confidence which lies behind this success is reflected in the extraordinary number of awards for finished work, and wins in competition, that the architects' record shows.

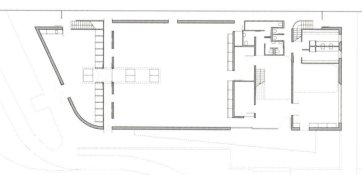

above: Nelson Court. The communal rooms are expressed at the corners.
plan: Nelson Court and the Drama Studio, ground floor.

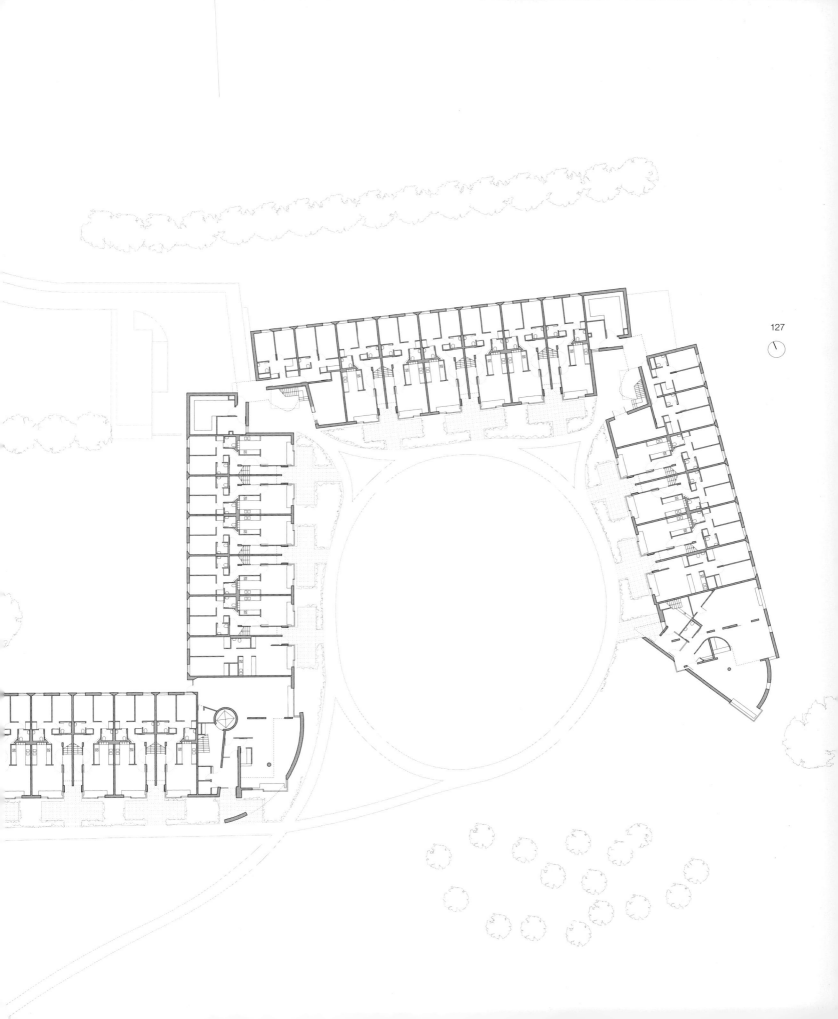

There are plenty of examples of this comprehensive approach in their other work; the proposed residential quarter in Central Milton Keynes, for instance. The commission is for a new sustainable residential quarter with supporting businesses and community facilities. The site will provide 2,400 new homes, and will be part of a wider strategy to redevelop the town centre. There is a benefit here from the growing appreciation of the complexity of cities, and how they work. To undertake what is in fact a mixed development, not just a housing estate, already represents a big jump onward from the post war approach to housing. The new quarter will provide the convenience and liveliness of urban living with good pedestrian access to public open space, the surrounding green space, and the nearby train station and town centre. This is very much in line with the original conception of Milton Keynes, which was a reaction to the way the new towns had been over-designed.

Accordingly, there is not only an area of housing, fairly conservative in layout, but paying attention to the division between frontage and backage, and making areas of semi-public open space as well as the public Grafton Park; there are also a number of commercial and office buildings, placed along the already defined main roads, and so reinforcing the city centre layout. Buildings are placed much closer to the roads than in the original plan by Llewelyn Davies and Weeks, giving more open space on the other side, where it can be used to conceal car parking, or for general amenity. This is the same policy that we noted in the case of Keble, where placing the new buildings close to the roads resulted in creating a new quadrangle. In this emphasis, Rick Mather Architects show themselves to be interested in improving public space, giving to new design some of the social qualities that make old cities enjoyable.

Residential Quarter Central Milton Keynes

Appointed by English Partnerships, the government's national regeneration agency, Rick Mather Architects are designing a new residential quarter with supporting businesses and community facilities in Central Milton Keynes. The 39 hectare (96 acre) site will provide 2,400 new homes and forms part of a wider strategy to redevelop the city centre. Milton Keynes was designed in the 1960s and built in the 70s as the country's first 'new city', the largest of the new towns. The site is positioned between the city's major shopping area and the main line railway station.

The scheme reconfigures the typical Milton Keynes block by building over the existing perimeter car parking

opposite above: Central Milton Keynes, Helmut Jacoby, 1971. Milton Keynes was designed in the 1960s, at a similar density to Los Angeles, in a time when the car was seen as one of the prime design factors. Central Milton Keynes was laid out on a grid pattern with the shopping centre at the lower end and the main railway station at the other. The site is outlined in red.
opposite below: The new masterplan proposes building more densely than originally envisaged to bring urban character and convenience to Central Milton Keynes.

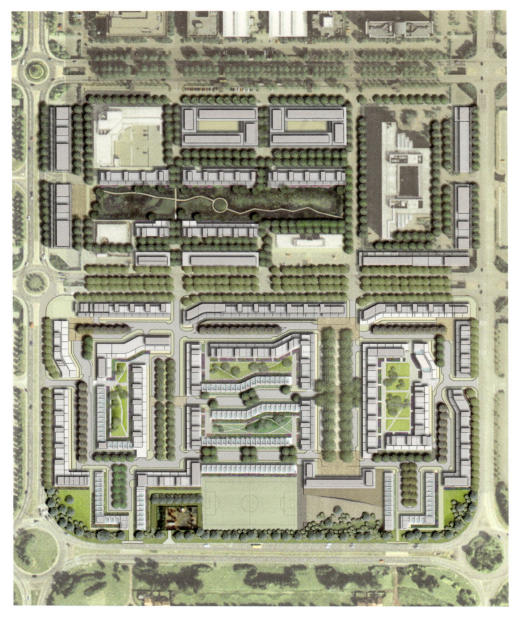

strip so that the new buildings define the edges of the main streets. This creates a much more urban street proportion where previously the buildings were too far apart to form a cohesive street. Locating development within the perimeter strip achieves a higher density, and the improved street proportions in combination with active frontages will help to encourage increased pedestrian activity.

The inflected forms of the buildings create vistas into the block and terminate the inner streets, which are conceived of as a series of places rather than corridors between buildings. This also creates a road layout that is naturally suited to traffic calming and is integral to the design of the scheme.

The landscaping and public realm incorporates differing species of planting, with seasonal variation for each group of streets and squares, called 'Character Areas', thus creating diversity across the block. The planting theme is carried through to the use of landscaped roof terraces and balconies.

left: The masterplan proposes a series of linked squares where buildings define space rather than acting as objects.
opposite: Homes for the Future, Glasgow.

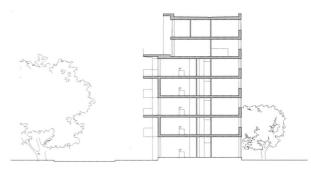

The housing at this stage is only sketched in. To have an idea of what it could be like we must turn to the scheme for Homes for the Future, a showcase residential development overlooking Glasgow Green. This project was conceived as part of Glasgow's 1999 Year of Architecture, and Rick Mather Architects were initially asked to design the central apartment block containing 24 flats and penthouses. On plan it is a fairly square footprint, facing south to the park, and the architects have seized on this frontality to make a striking design. The south-facing front is broken by a projecting access balcony at fifth floor level, which is known as a skydeck. Deck access used to be a tell-tale mark of public authority housing; here it is used to create a private realm, at a height that allows for spectacular panoramic views. This deck gives access to the penthouses, slightly set back, and broken up into pairs. Below are five floors of apartments, enlivened by a series of projecting terraces, each of which swells out to maximum depth and retracts at the ends. These projections are arranged in counterpoint, so that the whole facade is put into rippling motion. The construction was by design-and-build, so the architects could not prevent the balcony fronts being executed in wire mesh, whose vertical supports diminish the movement imparted. Had they been carried out in solid concrete, as designed, the result would have been more substantial and to greater effect. Even so, they make an animated and attractive building. Characteristically, the other facades are quite sub fusc, but always carefully detailed. The back is just a back; the design effort has been put where it will have most effect.

Homes for the Future Glasgow

Playing a part in the regeneration of Glasgow's East End, Homes for the Future was the flagship for Glasgow's 1999 Year of Architecture. The boldly modelled sculptural facade of curving balconies faces south over the green towards the River Clyde, while the rear elevation overlooks a new landscaped urban square. Above the balconies, a skydeck bridges to the neighbouring building and provides panoramic views for the two and three bedroom penthouses.

The flats have a minimised depth with a maximised undulating frontage to make the most of the southern aspect. Large open plan kitchen/living/dining areas look out onto Glasgow Green. The balconies follow the undulating plan of the apartment, and by offsetting one plan above

Homes for the Future, Glasgow.
above: Section: top floor duplex flats above three floors of one and two bedroom flats, above retail space.
opposite above: Skydeck looking south-west.
opposite below: Plans: top floor; fifth floor; typical floor; ground floor.

another create a simple but effective play of pattern light and shadow. They also serve to direct internal views away from adjacent flats. Each penthouse flat has a series of sliding screens that open out onto the skydeck. Formed entirely of galvanised metal with cedar decking, the skydeck runs the entire length of the building at fifth floor level. Skydeck spaces are generous enough to be used as external rooms served by the living areas.

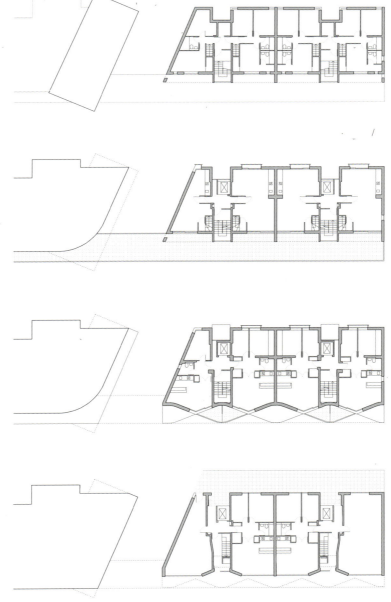

The Times Newspaper Headquarters, Wapping

This office building, east of Tower Bridge, fills the site to its limits to reinforce the line of the surrounding street patterns and link with the scale and height of the adjacent buildings. The normal storey height is reduced by eliminating the need for ceiling voids to help give a high site density without having to resort to tower or 'stand alone' building.

On the deep irregular shaped site a landscaped central courtyard allows the building to be narrow enough for good natural light and cross ventilation through opening windows.

The projecting triangular windows are etched on one side to direct views towards the street and not the adjacent residential building. The ground floor facades are fully glazed to give an active frontage to the street. The glass undulates on the uphill side to make space for vents from the parking below.

The building was given a 'BREEAM' audit to assess the level of environmental considerations in its design, construction and maintenance and received the best rating of any office building in London.

136

The Times Newspaper Headquarters.
opposite: First floor plan and north-south section.
above: The main elevation at dusk.

The talent to design a single building, of course, is the *sine qua non* of the successful architect. Sometimes, a building is just a building. This limitation will undoubtedly apply to Rick Mather Architects' design for The Times Newspaper Headquarters in London, close to Tower Bridge. As befits a newspaper office, however, it is an eye-catching exercise.

The building is of seven storeys, but the top floor is recessed behind a balcony front, exposing the outer edge of the butterfly roof, which thus takes on the weight of a cornice. But it remains primarily a roof overhang, as is shown by its perforations, three metre (ten foot) circles cut out of it at regular intervals, two per structural bay. Below, the main facade is subtly cranked, so that it meets the adjoining frontages squarely, while the concrete frame which holds up the building is set orthogonal to the volume behind. The result is a play of solid and void, as the columns, concealed at the west end, emerge gradually to represent the building fully at the east end.

A glass panel rises from the canopy the full height of the facade, leaning forward rather ominously as if to check your entrance, but in the end, as it is motionless, no more threatening than a banner. The glazing along the whole of the ground floor waves as it goes (the bulges reveal the smoke vents from the basement car park). Everything shows an interest in form, in making a play with form, exceeding what simple functionality would have dictated. For a newspaper office, it goes far beyond the simple signs that publicity would require, but in doing that it sets up a situation where we are no longer interested in the status of the owners: we have moved into architecture.

This is confirmed when we examine the rear elevation. It angles outward in plan, providing a deep volume, and the angle is reflected in the boxing out of the windows on a triangular system, so that one side is parallel to the orthogonal structure. They take in ample light, but for privacy concerns, are etched on the sides that face a nearby residential loft. They are not continuous, but spaced out on a brick wall. Only on the end gable wall do we find some orthodox strip windows, again set into the

ISMA Centre
University of Reading

In February 1995 Rick Mather Architects were asked by the University of Reading to design a teaching facility for the Zurich based International Securities and Markets Association (ISMA).

The ISMA Centre, through its open and transparent interior, is a clear spatial interpretation of the client's wish that the building's occupants interact. The brief was for a highly distinctive modern building which would reflect the type of research and work being carried out. The large areas of internal glass are intended to mimic those commonly found in City institutions where dealing floors are highly visible.

Open plan offices around a double-height common space, and the absence of corridors, encourage people, ideas and information to mix and avoid an institutional feel, an aim which the client expressed at the outset. The large glazed facades make best use of pleasant views to the north, and of the sunny terrace

ISMA University of Reading

brick facing. The relatively small windows were part of the energy strategy. Careful low-energy design has enabled the development on a relatively deep site to be naturally lit and ventilated, with savings in storey height which produced a bonus of an extra office floor. The building thus gets every inch of office space out of its site, but looks as if this aim never came into consideration.

However, the example which really turned me on was the ISMA Centre at the University of Reading. This is a commercial building only in the sense that it is a school for training dealers; as a school, it is also a part of an academic community, and this is reflected in its face, which is proudly turned to the front and looks suitably grave. Indeed, with its high overhang, it even has a touch of a pilgrimage chapel about it! The overhang shelters the terrace in front of the building, and since there is a coffee counter just inside, it serves in fine weather as a pavement cafe. The coffee counter is also a bar, and, no doubt as part of the pursuit of business success, it sells a lot of champagne. Behind, there is a double-height room that extends through to a large window to the north which has a marvellous view of leafy parkland. To the east is the glass wall to the mock dealing room. There is a lift to the working floor above, but students are asked to take the stairs just left of the entrance doors: a representation of the first flight is given on the exterior: so this is seen as an important path. The lift is detailed as a high tech icon, glass cage in a glass enclosure, immaculate white metal, silent action: an embodiment of Cedric Price's dictum of "well-serviced anonymity".

On the first floor, the administration is located on the balcony above the entrance where one person checks the circulation on through to the right hand bay, where the computers are set out: this is where the individual teaching takes place, on computer. This teaching space is lightened by a roof light along its whole length, so there is a diffused general daylighting that doesn't compete with the light of the screens. At the same time, the large windows to both north and south ensure that one doesn't feel cut off from nature, and the close carpet is a sage green that feels like a lawn. The internal structure consists of circular smooth concrete columns of about 20 centimetres (eight inches) diameter, which offer the slightest possible impediment

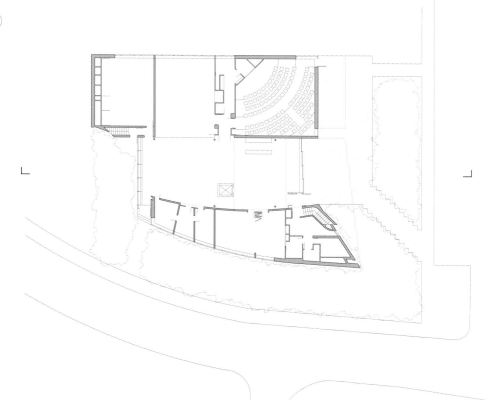

to the south. The first floor level is predominantly open plan, naturally lit from a linear roof light running the length of the building. Ground and first floors are linked by a glazed lift within the central common area. At the diagonally opposite corners of the building the staircases are expressed in the external facade. The dominant expression of the external envelope is of the two accommodation blocks arranged either side of the transparent, glazed double-height communal area.

The building defines a prominent corner on a major route into the campus. The curving road defines the site's west perimeters. The solid west wall follows and expresses this boundary and is drawn to a point at the building's south-west corner, enclosing the paved terrace. The pitch of the roof follows the gentle slope of the site.

left: Plans: first floor; ground floor; section north-south.
opposite above: The common room with its quiet parkland view. The dealing room is through the glass screen to the right.

to the flow of space. So a certain enjoyment ensues, an enjoyment of the fact that entrance, administration, and teaching are all part of one big space that rolls through the entire building, all beautifully detailed, as if a life in business were the modern equivalent of a life of virtue.

Walking around the building, which is faced in long, thin yellow bricks, some laid vertically to emphasise the curved surfaces, the same feeling of well-serviced anonymity comes to mind, although there is also a certain play of chance about the way the various windows are arranged. The mood is low-key, as befits a back. But, returning to the front, one is wowed by the serenity of the terrace area. And then one notices that the roof overhang is broken halfway along, presenting a view of its chamfered section, and by its division articulating the two major spaces behind. This detail is very important, not only as a form of expression of the plan, but as a way of lightening the parti, and breaking up the building mass. Without that break in the roofline the building would be a monolith, it would lack something, it would be less human. A certain joy entered my heart. As a critic, I felt seriously engaged by that detail; I felt justified in writing this book.

And I began to think of Mather not simply as a superb designer, but as a serious architect: one who has reached a level of working with the brief, and going beyond that to take issue with architecture as an art. A certain meditation about not only the role of the building, but also the role of the architect. Could it be that, unlike what I had believed at the outset, Mather was a Mannerist? He might not be happy to be so identified, but for me, it would be the highest of compliments.

After all, there is nothing in the brief that justifies writing the first flight of the stairs as a sculptural projection on the outside of the building. That must come from an entirely different motivation. Now, I would have to go back over all the examples I had already characterised as simply good design, and see if this extra dimension could be identified.

Come to think of it, The Times Headquarters could easily be assessed as Mannerist. There is a delicate balance between the orthogonality of the structural frame and the slightly different angle of the street frontage, which is a problem to be solved only if one is alert to the formal consequences and possibilities that may be involved. The gradual emergence of the trabiated facade allows a balance between two contrasting treatments. To make what is quite an elaborate game out of it seems to indicate that gamesmanship is part of the situation. How did this problem arise? It may have been prompted by sheer empirical pressure, but it seems to have been sublimated into something more cerebral, something that can be enjoyed by those who know, without interfering with the way the building is taken up by its users. Other details of this design, like the angled windows of the rear elevation, or the angled panel hanging above the entrance, are at least unusual.

Going back over the other cases that we've examined, with this new interpretation in mind, other possibilities open up. For instance, at Keble: it's clearly not a pastiche of mid-Victorian architecture, but neither is it an example of unabashed Modernism, as at Lincoln. So, it's something that lies between, a Modern building that stays within limits. It pays close attention to its context. There is no elaborate game with stripes,

above: Sloane Robinson Building, Keble College, with one-piece frameless glass entrance canopy.
opposite: ARCO Building, Keble College. Similar coursing details and window type unite the buildings around the garden.

but the storey heights are marked by a course of not coloured but simply recessed bricks, and this at least underlines that the scale is similar to the old. Yet on the main facade of the Sloane Robinson Building, one realises that the recessed bricks are not placed at the floor levels, but at window sill levels. They are really a marker not of structure, but of scale. This becomes quite clear when we notice that the line runs out against the reveals of the main windows. So it was a subtle sort of decoration, not a constructional floor marker. It doesn't strike us as mannered architecture, but it is certainly thoughtful.

And at Lincoln, where the Modernity seems quite unabashed, it is still an extraordinary thing to see how the overhang of the fourth floor at the east end comes to a stop exactly on the corner of the building, so that corner of the lecture theatre runs up in an unbroken line to the top. Having to think about that, one comes to feel that it is not simple structural need that makes the cylindrical columns under the lecture theatre just noticeably fatter than the run in front of the foyer, but an enjoyment of a disparity. It makes the lecture theatre its own master, and the long facade becomes a combination of two structures. Again, it's not Mannerism, exactly, but it is very considered.

What seems on reflection to go beyond simple functionality is the handling of the entire staircase. The landings that bridge between the two sides are finished in a dark colour, where the balustrades are in white concrete. There are just three colours, the landings, the balustrades, and the stone of the steps. The result is to create an abstract pattern that dances in the mind. It is like achieving decoration out of purely functional elements, but going beyond use into a kind of fantasy. It brings a greater enjoyment, without spending more money.

Lincoln School of Architecture.
opposite: A simple palette of materials accentuates the play of light within the atrium.
above: The atrium opens south to a terrace and in the future will overlook the pool.

Going back to The Priory, one becomes aware that here there are multiple possibilities for this new interpretation. We've already noticed a general awareness in this building of historical precedent—the tradition of white-walled villas that Le Corbusier set off with the Villas Stein and Savoye—and we've discussed how the building plays with a flow of space from the top down, and from side to side, one direction based on the main axis from the front door, the other from the main living room window and its adjoining roof light facing south. These two movements are both strong, and one can feel almost dizzy with the movement of space and light. Yet, there is a sufficient area of blank white wall to hold on to, to check the dizziness. The abstract forms are in a delicate equilibrium, just as we are suspended between the sharp edges of the glass balustrades and their precision in defining the geometry. I hadn't thought of all this as Mannerist, but it certainly brings to mind the play of ambiguity frequently to be encountered in Mannerist architecture.

And we did also notice a play of narrow slots of glazing, introduced to clarify the massing and the limits of the masses. For example, where the bather passes momentarily through a visible zone, the owner insisted on this glass being etched, which in a way spoils the game—but, as noted, the slot still works to make one aware of the spatial hierarchy. I thought that the complexity and ambiguity created by the use of glass, including its use for the stairs and for parts of the floor, were certainly mannered, but perhaps had more to do with angst and the search for conceptual clarity. If this, again, is not exactly Mannerism, it may be its equivalent in our age of anxiety. Ever since Colin Rowe wrote *Mannerism and Modern Architecture* this conjunction has provided a general possibility for interpreting Modern architecture, and it certainly comes to mind in dealing with Rem Koolhaas, whose work seems to be a continual reinterpretation of the forms of the heroic period, particularly as employed by Le Corbusier.

The Royal Horticultural Hall seems to be very straightforward in its dealing with a period building: the order is reinstated, the additional Modern space created is distinct from the old, and the combination seems rational without being too concerned about

The Priory, Hampstead. Top floor.

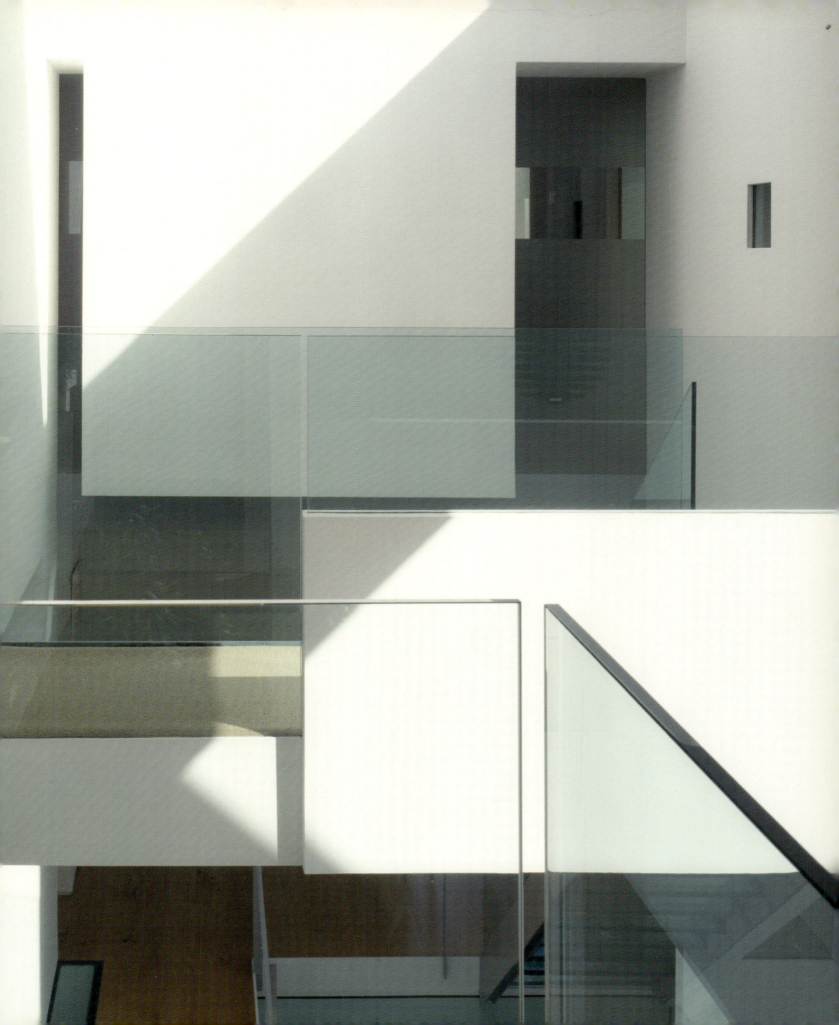

opposite above: Dulwich Picture Gallery, after Second World War bomb damage.
opposite below: The Mausoleum.
above: Breakfast Parlour, Soane Museum, Lincoln's Inn Fields.

conflicts of interpretation. There is a subtlety about the external appearance, where the structural lattices are given a gentle curve towards the base, and this certainly mixes in an element of 1900 with the Modern features, but I would hesitate to call it Mannerist. It certainly doesn't seem to be concerned with expressing angst.

But what about Dulwich? That is a case of a building very much together, it is surely a direct expression of its author's preferences. What does it tell us? To start with, Soane was himself something of a Mannerist. The famous hanging arches in the dining room of the Soane Museum came long before Venturi employed the same idea above the staircase in his National Gallery extension at Trafalgar Square. Structural ambiguity is ambiguity, but it doesn't necessarily imply a Mannerist intent. Soane is usually designated as a forerunner of Modernism, largely due to the way his pendentive arches, meeting on the supports at a point, create a flow of space. The most powerful expression of this was in his remodelling of the Bank Stock Office (unfortunately demolished in 1930), but it's an idea he used frequently, and can still be seen at Pitzhanger Manor, and in the Breakfast Parlour in the Soane Museum. As someone who was active at the moment when Neo-classicism was just giving way to Romanticism and the Picturesque, Soane is full of piquant contrasts, that may arise

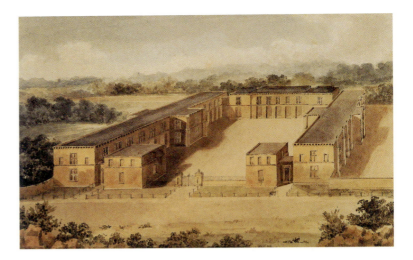

more from his temporal context than from introspection. Yet he was, undoubtedly, a thoughtful architect, a man of poetic vision. And there is something mannered about his obsession with crowding his antiquities into a space too small for them, and at Dulwich about the details of the mausoleum. This is an unusual combination of a circular colonnade and a Greek cross, jammed together in a Beethovian way, yet through the handling of light, imbued with poetry. On the outside, the primitivist simplicity of the brick piers and recessed entablature is offset by the elaborate incisions on the lantern, flanked by no less than three sarcophagi, each with an impossibly compressed pediment, and surmounted by five identical urns, one at each corner and one on top. The fact that they are identical may show that we have already entered the era of mass production, or it may be due to Soane's poetic sensibility. As always, we are left in some doubt.

And we are left in some doubt about Mather's intentions, in building hard up against such a prestigious predecessor. The idea of building a quadrangle in front of the gallery was, of course, in Soane's original intentions. There is nothing outlandish in that. But there are certainly other aspects worth commenting upon. The bronze 'ladders' outside his structure have weathered to a distinctly mottled surface, which gives them the air of being made by an artist, not by a high tech architect. Although the real structure is clearly high tech, and the glass windows uncompromisingly Modern, the final effect is much more human, and in terms of addressing itself to the user, more lovable. Is this Mannerist? Not exactly, but insofar as the final state of the bronze could not be predicted accurately, it was optimistic.

The ways in which these additions match Soane's own method seem to be based on common sense: the hiding of the additions behind a featureless brick wall is an act of discretion, and if it makes the need for top lighting, as with Soane, this appears as a natural contemporary ploy, not as a search for complexity. In fact, Mather always ends up with a deceptive simplicity, rather than evident complexity. His work does not induce anxiety, it reassures.

Then there is the Homes for the Future, at Glasgow. I wasn't able to get inside the apartments, but perhaps that wasn't necessary. This building puts all its eggs in one basket, and that is the elevation towards Glasgow Green. It is a rippling facade that affects the whole building, a tour de force. If this is Mannerism, it is not the expression of angst, but of a kind of enjoyment of life. It is more like what John Shearman, in his book *Mannerism*, 1967, defines as "the stylish style", conceived of in the spirit of virtuoso performance. He says:

> [In Mannerism] we may look for developments that exceed the norm in respect of refinement, grace, complexity, demonstrative accomplishment, or caprice. An obsession with style may again triumph over function; at first sight this point promises to be clearer in the case of architecture, an essentially functional art, than in painting or sculpture…. What matters, then, is the visual effect—whether it is of style in the service of a functional idea, or of style so emphatic, so autonomous, that justification by apparent function does not arise.

opposite: Dulwich Picture Gallery. Design numbers four and five, Soane Office, 1811, showing Soane's intention to create a courtyard in front of the gallery.
above: Homes for the Future, Glasgow.

Mannerism began as a virtue, the pursuit of high excellence, entirely admirable; but it quickly became suspect because it suggested and seemed to require artifice, and this change happened towards the end of the 1500s. In so far as it was practised, and largely invented, by Raphael and Michelangelo, it was initially inseparable from the High Renaissance. Subsequently, in the attempt to rescue sixteenth century art from the ill repute that much of it enjoyed in the nineteenth century, it has been endowed today with virtues peculiar to our times—especially the virtues of aggression, anxiety and instability. Shearman will have none of this. He rejects the twentieth century interest in interpreting Mannerism "in terms of tension, reaction, irrationalism or crisis, and the tendency to see [in it] an intention to shock in a discomforting way". This puts paid to our suggestion that, in The Priory, the play of glass balconies had something to do with angst. Mather was not attempting to shock us. But he was showing off.

It leaves the possibility that there is in Mather an interest in virtuoso performance, or at least in "demonstrative accomplishment". In its sheer exuberance, the facade at Glasgow seems to embody this intention. This building does more than provide housing, it exceeds the norm in respect of refinement, grace and complexity and so comes to make a statement about the power of architecture.

The Dulwich Picture Gallery Mausoleum, for the original donors.

Urvois House
Holland Park

A detached classical nineteenth century house on a wide street in a leafy neighbourhood, where the existing house had many problems—badly built extensions, a wasteful plan and a recent, ill-conceived renovation—but great potential. The interior was stripped out, staircases relocated, redesigned and made new, and the back extension redesigned and rebuilt giving the clients more space than they ever imagined possible.

The house is in a conservation area in Holland Park, London, therefore all alterations to the outside of the house were restricted. From the front the only sign of difference are the plants of the roof terrace. Having gutted the interior a central four-storey structural glass stair was inserted below a new large and fully opening roof light, allowing daylight

Urvois House, Holland Park.
The garden level swimming pool with natural light filtered through the glass staircase and fibre optic 'stars' in the ceiling.

Maybe there is a connection here between the reverence due to an institution, and the freedom that might be acceptable in working for a purely private client. After completing The Priory, the same team was put to work on an interior for a house in Holland Park. This is an early nineteenth century classical house, of four storeys. The architects have gutted the shell completely and put in an entirely new interior. In the lowest floor, level with the garden, as at Hampstead, is a swimming pool, and daylight does indeed reach it via a new large roof light. The roof light comes directly above the stairs, admitting light all the way down. But the interest focuses here on the staircase itself, which, with its carefully designed glass balustrade, is clearly intended to offer the least possible obstruction to the flow of light. The balustrade runs up the whole height halfway between the two flights of stairs, and is supported by metal spacers off the stair carriages. The individual steps are also of glass, and the space between treads is blocked (for Building Regulation requirements) by stainless steel rods tensioned from the wall. The result is that light really does come down the staircase to the pool, which also receives light from the large windows to the garden.

156

to flood down through the entire house. A double-height glazed structure was added to the rear of the house linking the living space to the garden. The glazing is protected from thermal gains by automatic external roller blinds installed with sensors to close in the event of rain.

At ground level the swimming pool and family room open on to the terrace and garden. On the first floor the living and dining spaces open into the glazed rear addition. On the second floor the library and master bedroom both have cedar decks overlooking the garden. The third floor has four bedrooms with en suite bathrooms. Above there is a roof garden.

Urvois House, Holland Park.
opposite left: Plans: third floor; second floor; first floor; ground floor; west-east section.
opposite right: The glass staircase.
above: Street facade.

These windows face the rear garden, there is no hint of them on the front, and as they extend across the width of the house, they make the interior as a whole read as a Modern space. Yet they are divided into three bays, corresponding to the original plan of the house, the central bay being emphasised as a simple rectangular aedicule, two storeys high, finished in white plaster, that keeps the new glazing subsidiary to the old house. The living room on first floor level expands into the same space, for use as a dining area, and at the ends looks down into the garden floor, and is divided from it by a balcony edged with a glass balustrade, made from segments supported off the floor slab; but with the difference that some of these units are curved on plan. So there seems to be no constraint due merely to the use of glass. Everything falls into place without strain. The result is extraordinary, but not demanding. It will soon succumb to the pressures of daily life.

Yet the photographs that have been made, admittedly by a knowing eye, show a poetic use of materials used with such great simplicity that the details simply disappear, the sensuous experience comes to the fore, the effect is joyful. and not in any way expressive of angst.

above and left: The central glass staircase has a series of glass balustrades that tie one flight of stairs to the next.
opposite: First floor view from the living room through to the dining area.

@venue Restaurant St James'

The @venue was realised in the derelict shell of a former banking hall. The brief called for a restaurant to seat 170 people in as large and light a space as possible. To this end, the interior was stripped back to its structure, and the original roof lights reinstated.

The new facade is all-glass to engage the street, provide natural light, and views out from within the deep plan. The facade and roof light use frameless glazing for maximum transparency, helping to dissolve the division between inside and outside.

The kitchen and staff areas are located in the basement, and the air conditioning plant located in a new mezzanine floor above.

The white interior is set against a Spanish limestone floor, with the bar and built-in furniture in American cherry and steel panels.

So if Mather is a Mannerist, it has to be understood that it is only in the sense that he has followed superlatives in all his work. He does work from the brief, but he is alert to general effects that arise from the conjunction of the forms he uses. His sensitivity is such that almost any collision between elements can be turned to advantage.

This capability has enabled his practice to deal with a great variety of clients, from private individuals to august institutions. It is probably not an accident that they have made the transition from private to public largely through making restaurants: ZeNW3 in Hampstead, @venue in St James', Mirazur Restaurant on the Côte d'Azur, Zen Hong Kong. Restaurants have to be done with finesse, the more so when they have to carry a client's symbolism, like the water running down the plate glass balustrade in ZeNW3. But they are essentially for the public, and they are one of our main makers of public space, in an age when Trafalgar Square seems to be reserved for protest. Rick Mather Architects have done not one, but many, and they seem to have learned from doing them. They all carry the marks of a visual sensibility, and have become sought-after places to eat.

@venue Restaurant, St James'.
opposite: The main space, lit from a rediscovered and refurbished roof light.
above: The entrance inserted into the 1920s bank facade.

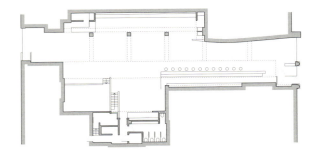

@venue Restaurant.
above: Ground floor plan.
left: Interior.
opposite: Mirazur Restaurant, Côte d'Azur.

Mirazur Restaurant
Côte d'Azur

Situated on the French/Italian border this 1950s tea room was remodelled to form a new restaurant, bar and private reception room seating 310 people. Overlooking its lemon grove are a new cocktail terrace and a covered timber deck. New outside stairs link down to the garden, and inside, a new spiral stair rises up from the bar and reception to the restaurant. High frameless windows fold back to panoramic views of the Mediterranean and the old town of Menton, or the high cliffs behind.

left: The existing building was opened up to the views and landscape.
opposite above: Views from the bar to Menton and Cap Martin.
opposite right: Plans: top floor street level restaurant; entrance, bar and kitchen level; north-south section.

165

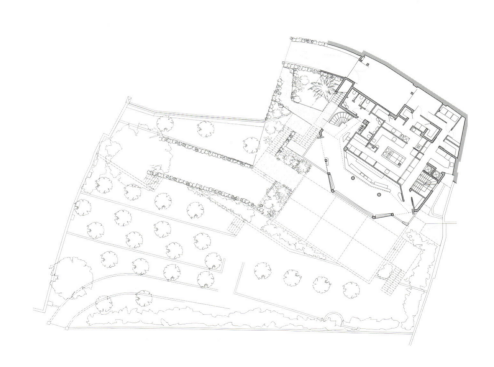

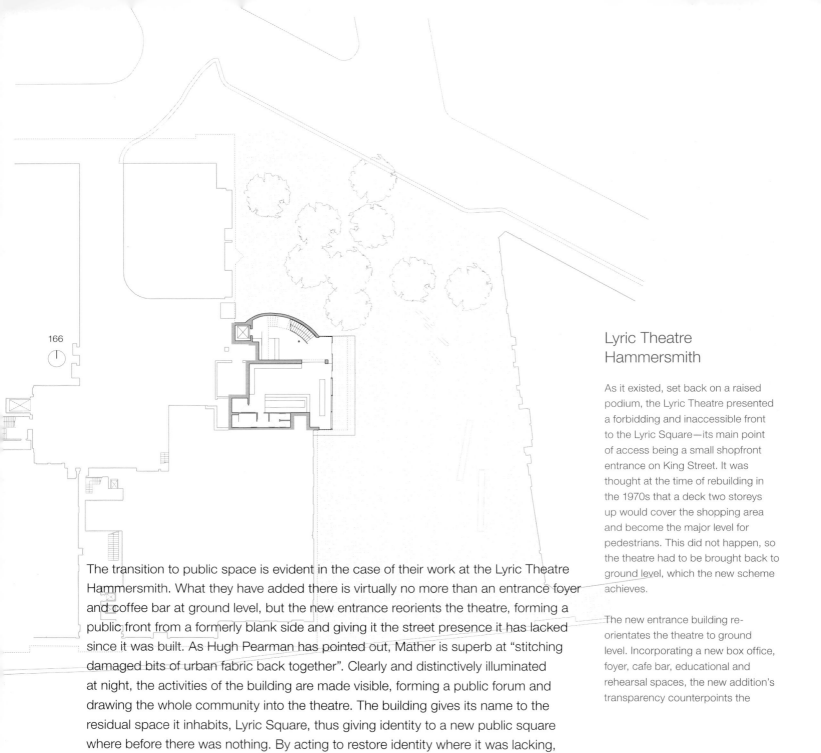

Lyric Theatre Hammersmith

As it existed, set back on a raised podium, the Lyric Theatre presented a forbidding and inaccessible front to the Lyric Square—its main point of access being a small shopfront entrance on King Street. It was thought at the time of rebuilding in the 1970s that a deck two storeys up would cover the shopping area and become the major level for pedestrians. This did not happen, so the theatre had to be brought back to ground level, which the new scheme achieves.

The new entrance building re-orientates the theatre to ground level. Incorporating a new box office, foyer, cafe bar, educational and rehearsal spaces, the new addition's transparency counterpoints the

The transition to public space is evident in the case of their work at the Lyric Theatre Hammersmith. What they have added there is virtually no more than an entrance foyer and coffee bar at ground level, but the new entrance reorients the theatre, forming a public front from a formerly blank side and giving it the street presence it has lacked since it was built. As Hugh Pearman has pointed out, Mather is superb at "stitching damaged bits of urban fabric back together". Clearly and distinctively illuminated at night, the activities of the building are made visible, forming a public forum and drawing the whole community into the theatre. The building gives its name to the residual space it inhabits, Lyric Square, thus giving identity to a new public square where before there was nothing. By acting to restore identity where it was lacking, Mather shows himself to be too concerned with amelioration to qualify as a Mannerist. Mannerism calls for a cold heart and artifice, where Mather imparts warmth.

On the same route to giving meaning to public space will be the Towner Gallery at Eastbourne, situated next door to the Congress Theatre (a Grade II listed building). Along with providing a home for the permanent collection, and a store for items not on display, it will provide conference halls, community activity rooms and a cafe. The exterior will incorporate a graphic display in the tradition of Terragni's Casa del Fascio at Como; in effect, more stitching together of the urban fabric.

Lyric Theatre, Hammersmith.
above left: Ground floor plan.
opposite: At night the new building acts as a beacon for the theatre's new ground level foyer, with views in to the new first floor education suite and the glowing top floor rehearsal room.

'fortress like' quality of the existing building. Clearly and distinctively illuminated at night, the building is the central focus for the new Lyric Square.

The new facilities provide a better environment for the development of artistic work to help to ensure that the highest calibre of artists continue to want to work with the theatre. The Lyric's education programme is improved with this dedicated and fully resourced room.

left: A rehearsal space sits over the education room and new cafe opening on to the new square.
opposite: Section; plans: first floor; second floor podium level. The new building provides a clear ground level entrance to the existing theatre two storeys up.

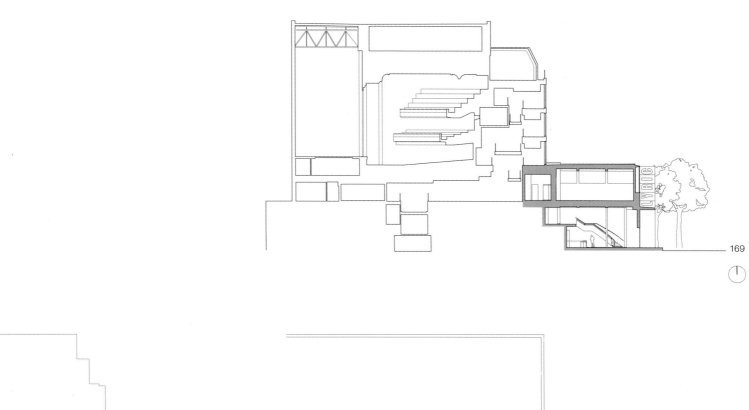

169

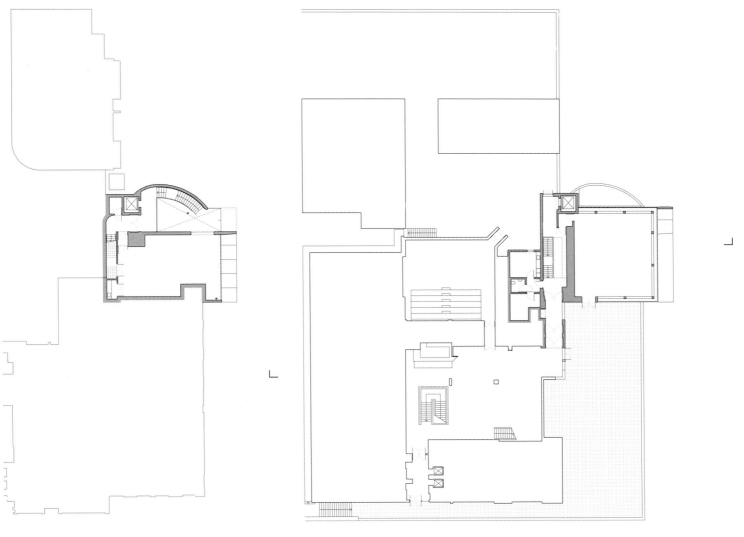

Eastbourne Cultural Centre

This major new public building is in a prime location next to the Grade II listed Congress Theatre and Devonshire Park, host to the pre-Wimbledon annual International Ladies' Tennis Tournament. The Cultural Centre provides a new home for the Towner Art Gallery collection, as well as a new conference space, shop and cafe.

The building incorporates easily accessible art storage for the Towner permanent collection to enable the public to view the gallery's entire collection for the first time. Flexible spaces have been designed to accommodate touring exhibitions,

Eastbourne Cultural Centre.
opposite: Eastbourne town centre, site of the new Cultural Centre (bottom left).
right: Ground floor plan, with the gallery's entrance. The new conference rooms behind link to the existing Congress Theatre next door.

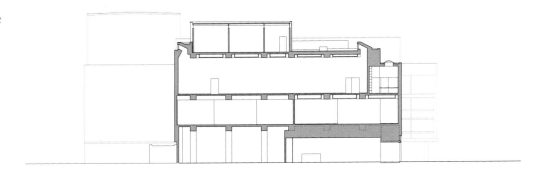

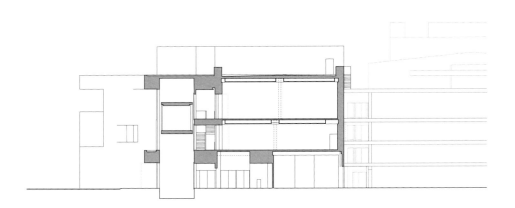

conferencing and the promotion of education and learning with the building acting as a base for community outreach programmes. The design of the new building is informed by many factors including views, circulation and the scale and nature of neighbouring buildings.

Conference and exhibition spaces are located at ground level with independent access allowing multi-functional use. Galleries are stacked vertically adjacent to the existing Congress Theatre, with connections between the buildings on all floors. These links encourage

sharing of facilities and the option to function together or independently as required. Community spaces and meeting rooms are arranged over the top two floors, with the cafe and roof terrace opening out to views across the South Downs to Beachy Head.

The solid metal-clad volume of the art spaces contrast with the transparency of the Congress Theatre. Fairface concrete finishes are used for the entrance area and canopy, and acrylic render is used on the remainder of the building, defining community facilities and the cafe to the west.

opposite above: North-south section.
opposite below: West-east section.
above: Eastbourne Cultural Centre, with Congress Theatre on the right.
right: Plans: second floor; first floor.

173

We have noticed one thing that might be related to the presence of Mannerism: the reference to historical precedent. Mannerism in principle goes with extreme self-awareness, with placing oneself within history. There is clearly in Mather an awareness of the history of the Modern Movement: Terragni, Le Corbusier, the emphasis on white walls that define the shape of the space and allow it to flow, the sensitivity to the play of light, the use of cylindrical columns, of double-curved walls, the transparency that is so assiduously cultivated—everything shows Mather to be before anything a Modern architect, to the point where no one would ever accuse him of being Postmodern. But surely he reflects closely on every detail, thinking not only of it as physical resource, but as part of the build-up of a mood. Doesn't this make him a complex designer, at least? Doesn't it remove spontaneity?

Here we are in a mystery. If not spontaneous, his style is singularly free, free from stylistic constraints, open to possibilities. Yet incredibly thoughtful, with minute attention to detail. I am tempted to apply a category of my own: the result with Mather lies always between two aspects that are separated by a hair's breadth: sweet disorder and the carefully careless.

I have written on this theme, because it seems to me that it is peculiarly apposite for architecture: one cannot do architecture without remaining in control, yet for architecture to reach the status of an art, it surely must encompass an element of spontaneity, a freedom of expression, such as the artist has conspicuously achieved. So if the architect approaches disorder, he must skirt it in order not to be sucked into the vortex; if he wants to stay in control, in order to manage the complex process of carrying out the building work, he must be careless only very carefully. In a way, Eisenman seems to be bent on showing that he can survive the vortex, but he does this only at some risk, and perhaps only because, like Libeskind and Rem Koolhaas, he is smart with words. Mather uses words not so much as part of his rhetoric, but for ordinary communication. He strikes one as "a forthright unassuming kind of fellow" (to quote Tracie Rozhon, who wrote about him for the *New York Times*). As an architect, he seems entirely bent on listening to the client, on understanding the client, on absorbing the brief, looking in it for an opportunity. In no way does he put the client through a wringer with no other purpose than to be able to express himself on the client's back: the self expression is there, but as a kind of subtext, muted, left for others to expose and comment upon.

So he tends to escape categorisation. One can make a case for The Times Newspaper Headquarters to be considered as Mannerist, one can make a case for the glass balustrades and the dizzy flow of space in The Priory to express a kind of angst: but these are interpretations put upon them, one can't be sure that they correspond to a truth. Any more than one can be sure of categorising Soane as a Mannerist; or Cockerell, or Lutyens, or even Venturi. These are all interesting architects, they were all extremely self-aware, their work is open to multiple interpretations. But they were all equally sure of themselves, and secure in the enjoyment of their skill. As is Mather. Which means that he may also turn out to have been, like them, great.

Louis Kahn proposed to divide the architect's creative process into two stages. In the original, the visionary act, the architect consults his intuition: out of his rational knowledge of the brief, but even more out of his experience and meditative life, he is able to intuit the essential form of his building: what it itself 'wants to be'. Then comes a second process of design, a backwards and forwards process in which the initial form is subjected to pressures that arise from the attempt to conform in detail to the programme and to the client's needs. With Kahn, the first act produces a generic form, often geometrically pure; while the second, in which others may share, is a process of adjustment and 'complexification'. The resulting impure form is seen as more interesting than the pure form, not only because it bears the marks of life, but because the ideality of the original form acquires a strangeness through the more or less accidental distortions to which it is subjected.

This is an interesting proposal, directed at a general understanding of the subject; except that, with Mather, the concept behind the design does not emerge until he has started thinking about the problem. For example, the shape of the Design Academy is not around at the beginning, but emerges during the process. This would imply that Mather really has the confidence to come to his desk without having done the sketch on the back of an envelope. He may do that, but all in due course. To begin, he just opens the book.

So there is an initial confidence, that all will be well. It seems to conform with his optimistic stance, his general delight in nature, the cultivation of plants, the simple pleasure of light. Staircases that go up to the light, the light that falls on surfaces. A generalised *joie de vie*. Only thus can we explain the extraordinary enjoyment that his work seems to elicit, the munificence he dispenses in his development plans, the glad reception of his ideas. He is on the side of making things better, of a brighter future. Maybe that is the secret of his success.

Mirazur Restaurant, Côte d'Azur.
Cap Martin and 'Old' Menton in the distance.

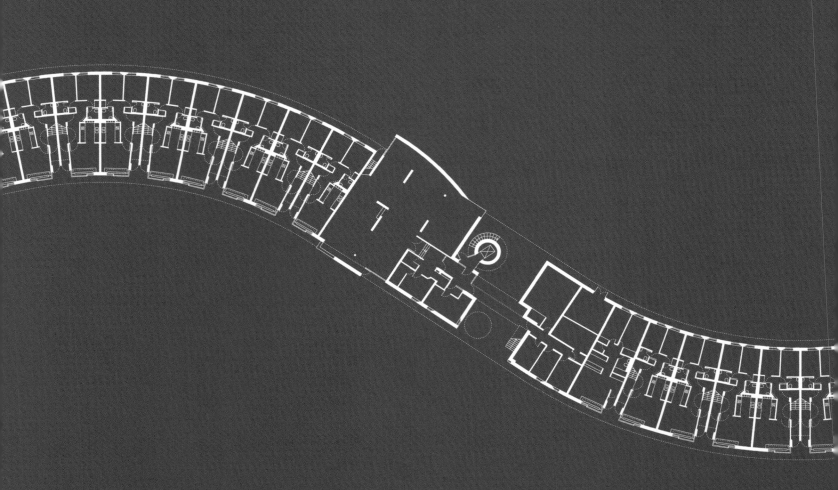

Optimising by Minimising
Tim Macfarlane

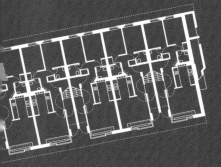

Ma & Pa Restaurant, London.
One of the first projects on which the
office collaborated with Tim Macfarlane,
and the first with Pat Carter, the builder.

The expressive steel and concrete structures that are often found in the work of engineers such as Felix Samuelly, Anthony Hunt and Peter Rice suggest a certain technical prowess where the boundaries of the technology are visibly challenged. Rick Mather Architects' architecture is rarely 'structurally expressive', though their pursuit of engineering refinement and their constant challenge to the norm have often stretched our engineering skills and structural materials to the limit.

Over 15 years of working together we have chipped away at structural member sizes and wrestled with squeezing out every bit of fat from our initial designs but the most surprising result is that we have been enticed into developing a whole new expertise in the design of glass structures and in the process encouraged the glass industry to build entirely new structures.

A central tenet of Modernism is the visible use of modern materials and technology. On the face of it, it would seem that a high tech building fulfils this requirement much more obviously than many of the buildings designed by Rick Mather Architects. It seemed fairly obvious in the late 1970s and 80s that engineers worth their salt were working on prestigious projects where the structural solution was articulated and celebrated at every opportunity. Peter Rice's approach for Le Grand Verre at La Villette, Paris, represents a high point in this movement and in Rice's oeuvre, and at first sight suggests significant glass engineering. On closer inspection it becomes apparent that the remarkably clever engineering is confined to the glass support system where the cable trusses fabricated from stainless steel rods and cast nodes are designed to minimise the stress in the glass. The rotule fitting which connects the glass to the truss was specifically developed for this project to allow the glass as much freedom of movement at the bolted glass connection as possible, thereby reducing the stress in the glass to a minimum. This may seem infinitely more complex and challenging than the 'all-glass' Hoffmann House extension. However, it is this project that represents a true leap forward in the use of glass as a structural material.

At a conference at The Bartlett School of Architecture, a well-known controversial teacher and critic accused Rick Mather Architects of mimicking a Modernist style rather than engaging with the real challenge of building with contemporary techniques. Our experience has been that on Rick Mather Architects jobs we are always challenged to think the unthinkable and design the structure to squeeze out every inch of material benefit. In the process we have learned that optimising by minimising the structure is significantly more challenging than expressing it. In the process we have developed a completely independent approach to glass engineering which has encouraged and allowed DMP to develop a similarly independent approach to glass design in the absence of national codes of practice.

Our first project with Rick Mather Architects was the Now & Zen restaurant in London, where a swooping fountain of crystal glass bowls suspended from the ceiling conveyed water from the upper mezzanine floor through the ground floor into the basement. Each bowl was shown on the concept sketch as supported on a single wire with no other visible means of support. Our first suggestion was to propose hanging each bowl from three cables connected to a common point on the ceiling. It transpired that Rick Mather had already designed such a fountain in a previous

Now & Zen, Covent Garden, London. Water runs through glass bowls with one support that sweeps down through the space from the roof to the basement.

restaurant for the same client and he now wanted to reduce the number of wires from three to one. We took a closer look at the problem and realised that we could treat the bowl as an upturned umbrella by introducing a short length of stiff rod at the bottom of the cable where it would be attached to the bowl through a single hole in the centre. The principle seemed straightforward and the only real issue would be, how long is the rod? As short as possible was the answer, and it was decided that as long as the rod extended beyond the centre of gravity of the bowl it would work.

As we were working to a tight schedule the 22 lead crystal bowls were made before we could test the hypothesis, but it was proposed that we carry out a test in any case before they were installed. A cable was duly fixed to the ceiling in Rick Mather's office and the rod was then bolted to the bowl and attached to the cable. A large black bucket was installed below the assembly just in case and Mather was called to witness the ceremony. Pat Carter, the contractor, climbed on to the ladder and commenced filling the bowl. At about half full the bowl suddenly tilted to the side and deposited all the water in the bucket.

Mather raised his eyebrows above his glasses, turned, and walked back to his office. Although he didn't say a word there was something about the gesture that inspired us to find a solution to the problem—failure to do so was not an acceptable idea. Fortunately that night, having drawn a full-scale drawing of the bowl, the answer emerged. The length of the rod had to be greater than the radius of the bowl otherwise it would tilt due to the uneven loading created by imperfections in the bowl's geometry, which would bias the load as it was filled with water. Although not a particularly useful bit of information for engineering building structures in general, the principle of thinking through a problem working from first principles to arrive at a simple and elegant solution became a hallmark of our work with Rick Mather Architects.

The pavement lights on this same project offered us our first real challenge in the design of structural glass. The idea was to find a way to bring as much natural light

Now & Zen, Covent Garden.
Large glass panels in the pavement light the basement dining space.

down to give the sense of a conservatory and not a basement, while offering the diners a view up to the passers by and vice versa. We contacted a well-known glass manufacturer and asked how this could be done. We were told that the largest sheets of glass they would use in this application were 75 centimetres (29 inches) square. Although this seemed to be a reasonable size to us, Mather was keen to have them as large as possible to emphasise the drama of walking across a bridge to reach the all-glass revolving doors of the entrance. We were faced with the challenge of how to engineer an external pavement light measuring 90 by 300 centimetres (35 by 118 inches), capable of carrying a point load of half a tonne (the wheel load from a full size truck), as well as supporting a crowd loading of five kilonewtons per square metre (104 pounds per square foot).

To be brought up in an era where all of the information necessary to design a steel, concrete, timber or masonry structure can be found in Codes of Practice is a mixed blessing. On the one hand the information is clearly documented and available, but on the other, the engineers who prepared the Code have carried out most of the basic thinking for you.

With glass there was no Code of Practice to consult, and in order to design the glass pavement lights we had to start from scratch. We began with the glass industry but to our dismay found that it was not at all easy to get them to part with even the simplest information such as the allowable tensile stress in glass.

Without some information about the physical properties of glass there was no chance of engineering a glass floor panel. There are invariably books that one comes across from time to time which seem to contain a disproportionately high percentage of useful information, and one of these for me is *Marks' Standard Handbook for Engineers*, a doorstop of an encyclopaedia covering all sorts of interesting topics, written on bible-thin paper and published in 1945. Although it seemed highly unlikely, there in the index was an entry for glass, and turning to page 647 I found two lines under the heading 'glass' giving all of the important physical properties for annealed glass including the indispensable tensile stress. It is hard to describe to the layperson how liberating having that number was and still is.

Of course having a number is one thing, but understanding what to do with it is another. I recognised that the tensile stress quoted was the average breaking stress for annealed glass subjected to load for a period of three seconds—this being the period that is used for assessing wind pressure when designing windows. We were designing a floor panel, and the load of five kilonewtons per square metre might need to be supported for a considerably longer period of time than three seconds.

I therefore decided in the absence of better knowledge to err on the side of caution, and used a safety factor of ten to arrive at an allowable tensile stress of seven newtons per square millimetre for the pavement lights. This required a single sheet of 19 millimetre (three quarter inch) thick annealed glass, which I then decided to laminate to another sheet of glass of the same thickness to provide a failsafe solution should either of the sheets crack. In fact, because the glass is supported on all four sides, both sheets of glass can break and the glass will remain in place and be capable of carrying the design load for a significant period.

Without contractors nothing would be built, and without exceptional contractors it is hard to achieve anything out of the ordinary. Pat Carter was the contractor on the Now & Zen restaurant and his experience with glass, and his introduction to the London glass fabricator FA Firman (run by the inimitable John Hodgson) were key to realising this design. The glass facade was also a challenge on this project and we were having some difficulty resolving the connection of the facade glass to the top of the revolving door. Pat is not someone to wait around too long on decisions that might prevent him achieving the opening date so, full of initiative as he is, he fashioned independently of the design team what became known as the 'toilet roll connection', which did the job structurally but was somewhat short of satisfying what I began to realise was the aesthetic of Rick Mather Architects. The revolving door itself was the first one to be made entirely from glass and is now much imitated. At that time none of the off-the-peg manufacturers would agree to produce the door. Carter said he would build it if the engineers accepted the design.

The Hoffmann House, our next job with Rick Mather Architects, was almost certainly the one that set us on a path to becoming known for our glass engineering internationally. Gaining planning permission for a modern addition to an eighteenth century listed cottage in conservative Hampstead posed a considerable challenge to the architects, and the confidence shown by Lord and Lady Hoffmann, the client for the project, in choosing an architect that would almost certainly refuse to resort to any form of Historicist conceit was well judged. In fact the planning approval may have been successful because being constructed entirely in glass, an ultra modern solution, it was hard to say that it had a style at all.

The design however did not start out as an all-glass solution. The first sketches produced by the design team defined the outline of a lean-to conservatory building which had frameless glass walls and roof, supported by half portal frames formed from steel pipe, with bolted connections supporting the wall and roof panels. It was clear from the sketches that the member sizes as drawn were woefully inadequate structurally and the bolted connections far too small as drawn. It was also clear

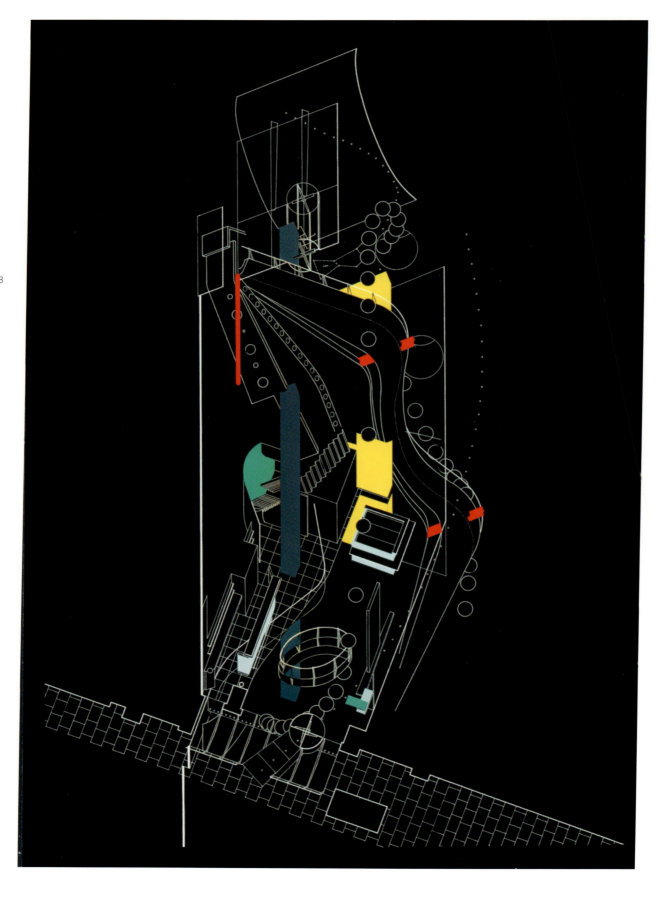

opposite: Now & Zen, Covent Garden. Axonometric drawing showing the constituent parts of the all-glass facade and first all-glass revolving door.
above: Hoffmann House, Hampstead. The entrance door is hinged off the house, with the kitchen to the left.

that Rick Mather wasn't happy to see anything larger and in a fit of rash inspiration I suggested that we could use glass beams. The speed and certainty with which Mather seized on this suggestion left me no room to back out, so I then embarked on a very uncomfortable two weeks of sleepless nights while I wrestled a solution out of the problem that I had given myself and he had locked me into.

As with the pavement lights for Now & Zen, laminating pieces of glass together to make a composite beam provided the answer; one piece could break and the other two would continue to support the roof. Connecting the roof beams to the external wall columns was, however, a further challenge, as doing so without bolts didn't seem feasible. Presenting the bolted solution to Rick Mather created the anticipated reaction and we were sent back to the drawing board, finally emerging with a mortise and tenon joint and no mechanical fixings.

As the extension is fully open to the remainder of the house, it was recognised that we would need to use insulated glass panels for the walls and the roof. Conventionally produced units are fabricated from two sheets of glass with an air space sealed at the edge using an aluminium spacer. A ten to 15 millimetre (a quarter to half inch) thick, dark coloured sealant completes the seal. Having removed the steel support beams we were now set the task of removing these visually strong lines at the edge of the glass. An extensive search revealed that Glasbau Hahn from Germany were the only company willing to produce a unit using glass spacer beads and a clear sealant material.

Although Glasbau Hahn is a reputable firm we were concerned that the unit might break down at the edges allowing moisture to leak into the air space. This type of failure results in fogging of the unit, which would be unacceptable. Fulcrum, the service consultants for the project, found heated glass panels produced in Finland, that had an invisible metal coating on the glass. A low voltage electric current is passed through the coating, which in heating up is designed to drive out any moisture that might accumulate. A surprising amount of heat can be generated using this

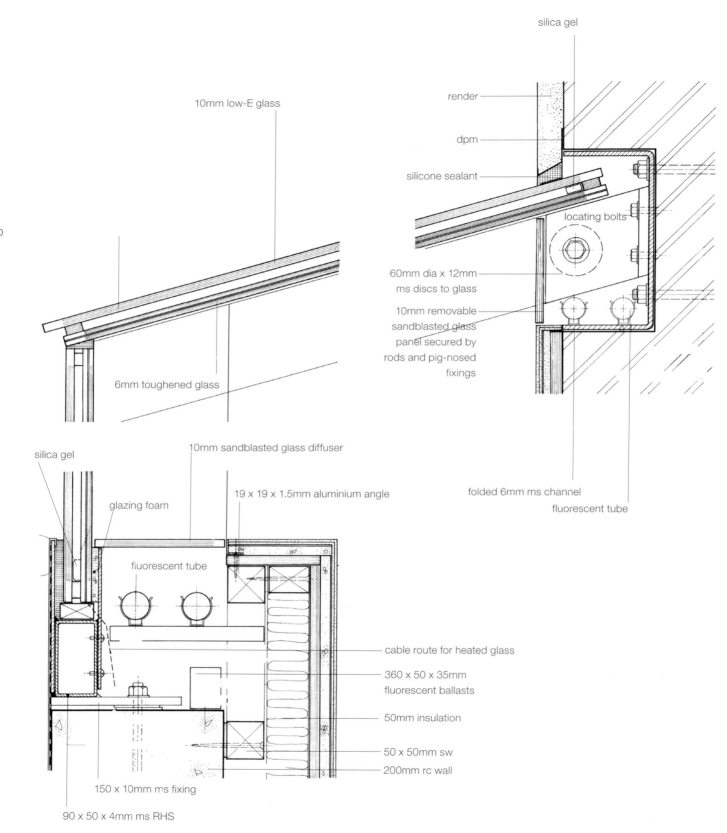

system; when the small 30 by 30 centimetre (12 by 12 inch) sample arrived on site for the design team to review, the contractor had plugged it in and was using it as a plate to keep his teapot warm. This demonstration was not lost on Mather, who then decided to eliminate the radiators he had designed for the space and to use instead the glass panels as the heat source. This arrangement has the advantage that the downdrafts associated with sitting too close to a window are eliminated. This small addition provided a vocabulary for working with structural glass that has been subsequently used throughout the world.

Building in the UK with a supportive private client is somewhat different from working in the United States on state owned buildings in a construction industry dominated by standard system solutions. Proposals for the Virginia Museum of Fine Arts, currently on site, included glass roof beams and glass bridges (that were omitted following a directive by the local building code official) and significant areas of 'frameless' external glazing. One 12 metre high by 22 metre long (40 by 72 foot) 'window' became the object of much debate. Glass walls of this scale have been built using glass fins in multiple pieces, clamped together with metal connection plates, bolted back to the external glass panels, and there is a desire within the local community to operate only within the confines of this 'closed engineered system' approach.

As with all our glass work with Rick Mather Architects, the goal was to eliminate the need for visible metal fixings. In response we developed the idea of using 12 metre (40 foot), full-height laminated glass fins to support the wind load, and designed the 3.5 to 4.8 metre (11 and a half to 16 foot) high glass wall panels to stack one on top of the other, using silicone spacer blocks. The face panels are held back to the glass fins using site applied structural silicone. Although this design is in principle extremely simple in concept and appearance, and has the support of each of the component manufacturers, it has proved exceptionally difficult to convince the state building code department, construction manager, the local design team and the client that the solution is structurally acceptable.

Hoffmann House, Hampstead.
opposite above: Detailed section at glass beam/wall junction.
opposite below: Detailed section through glazing base and roof.
This was the first example of an all-glass structure in the UK and looks deceptively simple. However, glass manufacturers were unwilling to take a risk in the making of such a structure at the time.

192

Glass engineering in architecture is 100 years behind steel and concrete. In the early twentieth century most of the frames that were being produced in these materials were licensed under patent to fabricators and the architect, whilst recognising steel and concrete frames would be the inevitable future structural form for building development, was frustrated by the lack of adaptability and choice in the industry. However, in response to demand the Association of Consulting Engineers was formed in 1906 and structural engineers joined the architectural design team.

Through time 'Codes of Practice' for these primary structural materials emerged which brought to the public domain knowledge that was hitherto the private property of the fabricator or patent holder. To engineers of my generation brought up with Codes of Practice to consult, it was hard to imagine a codeless period from 1906 to 1940 when consulting engineers were using their experience alone to produce economic steel and concrete designs specific to the architecture.

Knowingly or not, Rick Mather's relentless pursuit of glass solutions to articulate his very specific architectural expression has contributed to if not led to the forthcoming Code of Practice on Structural Glass.

When designing the glass beams for the Hoffmann House we approached one of the largest and best respected glass producers and fabricators in the world, and were told that the design we had produced was unsafe and should under no circumstances be built. It was a mark of Mather's intuitive understanding of the structure that this did not stop the process and after 15 years it is still functioning as designed.

From that experience it was clear to us that the glass industry was unhelpful and what is more didn't seem to know very much. With the benefit of hindsight we now of course recognise that the glass industry is a private concern with absolutely no obligation to share the extensive knowledge it has with the design team. If I were running a factory I would very much like to make the same thing again and again

Virginia Museum of Fine Arts. The 13 metre (40 foot) high picture window is the first use in America of a glass fin system on this scale.

rather than have to accommodate a new, even if better, idea for a one-off project. Repetition is more profitable than innovation.

However, progress happens on many fronts and as much as industry must constantly develop more efficient ways of making the best products that meet the market's needs, designers must constantly be thinking of new and better things to make: where this doesn't happen you have stagnation.

Rick Mather Architects' ongoing commitment to designing buildings in an environmentally responsible way raises the question of using glass extensively in the facade. The problem of heat loss and gain from a window wall needs to be accommodated by heating or cooling the internal space. The use of natural daylight is key to the success of many of their projects; however, the balance of glass with solid is carefully managed to maximise daylight but minimise the impact on the internal environmental conditions.

We have been wrestling with this issue of balance for many years and, as engineers known for our structural glass expertise, we are constantly being reminded by our environmental engineer colleagues that designing large expanses of glass is often environmentally unsound. Although the economic answer to this problem does not yet exist, the desire to solve it does and an answer will emerge. The idea of using a vacuum instead of an air space in an insulated glass unit occurred to us when we were working on the Hoffmann House project and although we weren't able to have such a unit made we have recently found a Japanese company that is producing them. The units are expensive but are capable of achieving an insulation value three times better than the best triple glazed unit with an overall thickness of just seven millimetres (a quarter of an inch). With a larger market and improvements in the production process this system will in time become economically viable.

The problem of shading is also being addressed by the development of coating technologies for large glass panels. Infrared mirror coatings (which are transparent to visible light) have been used in the industry for some time now and photochemical coatings designed to modify the remaining incoming radiation—visible light—are currently being developed, so it is conceivable that in the near future, environmental concerns will not be compromised by other design considerations.

The rigour Rick Mather Architects apply to exploring glass structures is also shown in their use of other, more familiar structural elements, such as steel, concrete, masonry and timber. The base structures we have designed for many of their buildings are often tightly controlled and a great deal of effort is expended to make a member 50 millimetres (two inches) thinner. Rather than assuming that Mather is being overzealous in pursuing a minimal structure we have come to appreciate the difference between, for example a 50 millimetre and a 32 millimetre (one and a quarter inch) handrail and its visual impact.

The staircase and bridge designs for Constable Terrace at the University of East Anglia, and the cloister structures for the Dulwich Picture Gallery, are good examples of expressed structures where the size of the structural elements is critical to the success of the design. Unsurprisingly, significant effort was required to refine the structure to achieve the desired result.

Rick Mather Architects' approach has always been to encourage and provoke the design team into reconsidering the obvious. In doing so, they stretch engineering to its limit and open the door to new possibilities.

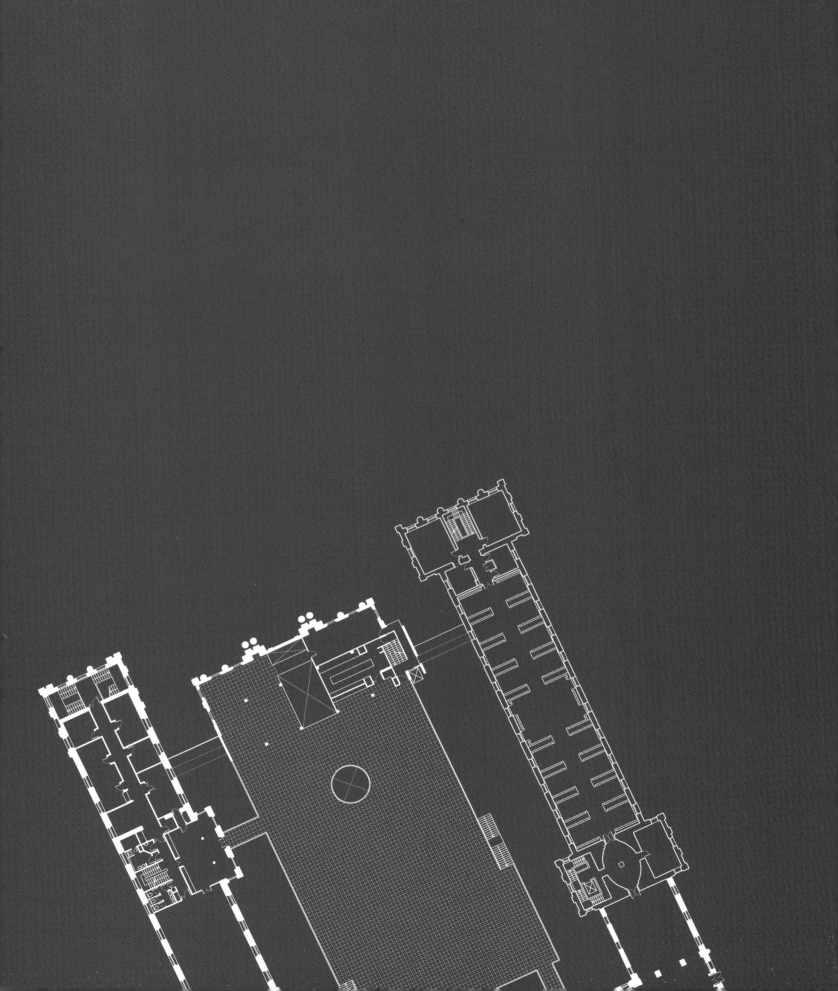

Environmental Design
Patrick Bellew

In the early part of the twentieth century Frank Lloyd Wright wrote extensive essays for *The Architectural Record* under the banner "In the cause of Architecture", in which he developed, among other things, an argument for 'organic architecture'. The term had a rather different meaning from that in common use today, as it described "an Architecture that develops from within in harmony with the conditions of its being as distinguished from one that develops from without". It referred to the thoughtful development of building plan, form and materials as a response to function, environment and need. This was, in part, a reaction to the burgeoning obsession with lightweight glazed facades after the First World War, as advancing technologies liberated architects from the restrictions of load-bearing elements, and Willis Carrier provided the means to meet the cooling loads thus created. Nearly 100 years later, the tensions between glass, architecture and energy still exist as points of debate.

Reading Wright's essays recently made me realise how the work that we have done with Rick Mather Architects over the years is from a very similar tradition; while the work of the office does not look 'organic' in the modern sense, there is a clear path in the process of design development of a collaborative journey where the elements are carefully constructed around environmental and structural conversations.

Sloane Robinson Building, Keble College, Oxford. South stair.

I first met Rick Mather at an environmental conference at the University of East Anglia (UEA) in 1993 where the practice had just completed Constable Terrace, the sinuous halls of residence that sit so artfully in the otherwise austere campus. His presentation on 'green' buildings started with the Now & Zen Restaurant, with its tumbling water feature and the glass conservatory in Hampstead. To this day I am convinced that he had picked up the wrong carousel of slides and was as surprised as we were to be presented with these images. His recovery however, with the description of the environmental principles behind Constable Terrace, was effortless—Andy Ford of Fulcrum Engineering engineered the building, and I think that even a decade later it stands out as a landmark scheme of its time. The guiding principle is the simplest of them all—conservation—the scheme values every watt in the way that Scandinavian designers had been doing for years.

As Mather unfolded the issues—super-insulation, controlled glazing areas, high performance glazing and heat recovery ventilation to recycle gains from students, lights and sun—it all seemed obvious and straightforward. Of course, it is not so; at that time those of us passionate about energy and resource conservation were struggling to persuade clients to move in this direction with only limited success. Natural ventilation was firmly believed by the majority to be the 'green' solution— ventilation without the need for fans being, wrongly in my opinion, touted as environmental Valhalla. What about all of the energy that goes out of the window to heat the cold air coming in? Why throw away all of the gains from people, lights and equipment on a cold day? And how much more air than you need comes through a window or vent when it is cold and blowing a gale?

My contribution to the conference dealt with many of the same questions and as we chatted over supper in the Sainsbury Centre I realised that despite my first impressions we were on the same wavelength. The shift away from a belief that natural ventilation holds all of the answers didn't really find the mainstream until several years later. Today the buildings that Rick Mather Architects were doing in 1994 have become more the norm.

The Priory, Hampstead.
The visual simplicity of the swimming pool belies the technical sophistication of the service solution.

It was a few weeks after the conference that I had a call from Rick Mather inviting us to collaborate on a house for a private client in Hampstead—The Priory. The house had a number of environmental features that stand out and represent the beginnings of the conversation that has developed over the intervening years. It mixes the ideas of high levels of insulation and heat recovery ventilation with controlled passive gains from sunlight, to begin to deal with the energy issues. The design also layers in complex natural daylighting through the house; at this time we relied on physical modelling to develop the design as the project pre-dated the availability of computer based daylight modelling tools by many years and was developed much more by instinct than would be the norm today. Indeed our recent work with Rick Mather Architects on the Ashmolean Museum has relied completely on 'Radiance' modelling to develop the daylighting strategies.

As the design for The Priory developed we began to understand the dedication to detail that is so much a hallmark of the work of Rick Mather Architects. At times it seemed to border on the obsessive but it was part of the learning experience for us to take the idea from Rick Mather to eliminate visible light sources and to work with the team to conceal them all in slots, returns and folds so that the light comes from everywhere and nowhere. The unheralded benefit of this move is that all of the lighting is achieved with very energy efficient linear fluorescent light sources as opposed to the plethora of energy consuming dichroic downlights which would otherwise have been the default design solution for this type of project.

The swimming pool is located in the lower ground floor of the house. To look at it is to look at what appears to be one of the simplest spaces in the house, but in practice the refinement and paring away of the detail to achieve this minimisation of the design took a huge amount of time and effort. Within the space, as well as the pool and a glass staircase, there is a warm floor, dehumidified air delivered from the ceiling and a high efficiency heat recovery unit which is concealed in a false wall and connected to intake and exhaust ducts which are routed vertically through the house to terrace and roof level.

The Priory has a large south-facing skylight that dominates the living space in the house and we had more than a few tussles about the potential for overheating as opposed to the benefits that it could offer for passive gains in winter and daylight through the house—Mather steadfastly maintained that if it got a bit too warm the occupiers could always just open a door at the top of the house that opens onto the upper terrace. This is what they do, and I hear that it works! Intuition sometimes beats numbers.

One wouldn't look at this house and immediately say that it is an 'environmental' building, as it doesn't have chimneys, funnels or grassy roofs. In the context of the period in which it was built it would have seemed to be far too Modernist in style to be seen as 'green' but, in the context of my opening 'organic' thesis every surface, opening, window and system has been considered for its environmental benefit in terms of heat, air and light flows and this ultimately defined the design. The stripping away of 'unnecessary' elements can be an alarmingly pragmatic journey of minimisation and reduction that does leave a very clean and efficient result.

There is no doubt in my mind that synthesis and reduction of these variables led to the development of a richer and more refined architecture. The arrangement of rooms in the house harks back to Vitruvius and his *Ten Books on Architecture*, where he wrote about the proper exposures of the different rooms and began to define the relationships between architecture, climate and comfort. The master bedroom faces to the east and living spaces face predominantly to the south and west.

This is not to say that this building, or any of the buildings that we have developed with Rick Mather Architects' office, are necessarily fully optimised paragons of environmental virtuosity but they do represent a significant step away from the Modernist exclusion of environment as a key driver or variable in the design process. Here for us were the beginnings of an inclusive design process that we were able to develop through the latter part of the 1990s with the office. Today this process has become the norm for the vast majority of projects, in name if not always in deed, but Rick Mather Architects were certainly in the vanguard of this environmental Modernist thinking.

Despite numerous trials and tribulations getting the house commissioned, built, and completed, it went on to win numerous awards and was runner up for the Stirling Prize, which was celebrated at a very exciting but rather hot RIBA on the night that Foster and Partners won the award for the Duxford.

We started design work on the @venue restaurant some time after the Hampstead house but, as is the way with these things, it was completed in 1995 well before The Priory was on site. The @venue was a different scale of undertaking, to provide an 180 plus cover restaurant and full kitchen in a basement on what was quite a small site, albeit with very high ceilings. Here again the emphasis of the developing design was on light and minimisation—it is virtually impossible to discern how or where air enters the space from anywhere in the room and the systems are folded away into tiny spaces like the pieces in a Tetris puzzle.

As I recall, the client, Chris Bodker, placed great emphasis on achieving excellent air quality in the restaurant. The problem was to get the air to all corners of the restaurant and bar, beneath myriad beams, without spoiling the height of the space. The simple solution that was arrived at was to route the ducts and other kit from end to end of the space above the bar, to float a layer of ceiling below them and to place a precisely dimensioned full height mirror at the far end of the Dining Room that aligns precisely with this ceiling. This draws the eye into the far distance and turns a bulkhead into an integral part of the interior design.

The @venue was built by a specialist shop fit-out contractor called Pat Carter. Carter is a unique man and we have had the good fortune to work with him on a number of projects, ten years on and the space still looks great—a testament to enduring architecture and high quality construction.

In 1996 we were interviewed for a project at Keble College in Oxford to provide a new residential, seminar and conference centre in the grounds of the old college. Rick Mather Architects had just completed the adjacent ARCO Building and had almost immediately been asked to expand the complex further.

@venue Restaurant, St James'.
The introduction and removal of air into the main space does not interrupt the clean lines of the design.

The competition, which took the form of a submission and interview, was run by the then Bursar of the college, Ken Lovett. We were delighted to win and Ken became our client on this project and later for the Ashmolean Museum. Ken died in 2005, but he remains in memory as one of the most exceptional and enlightened clients that we have ever worked with.

The building is part residential and part academic, comprising a large lower ground floor auditorium sunk deep into the ground, seminar, music practice rooms and a refectory on the middle floors and two levels of en-suite bedrooms on the uppermost floors.

The context of the building was vital to the development of the design. The site is on the perimeter of the college with adjacencies to the original late nineteenth century buildings designed by William Butterfield, and to a major extension by Ahrends Burton and Koralek (ABK) dating from 1979. Rick Mather Architects' ARCO Building sits on the other corner of the site. The new building was effectively to form a new courtyard bordered by these neighbours, and in particular was limited in height to that of the historic buildings. Originally intended for 'gentlemen wishing to live economically' it is particularly apposite that the modern buildings at Keble should be environmentally fastidious.

The technical and spatial challenge in the project ultimately came down to fitting in an expanded brief (the common room was extended to a 150 seat lecture theatre and a dining room was added), while keeping within the constraints set by the planning permission that was already granted. There was also the small problem of locating the large column free volume of the main lecture theatre on the lower ground floor.

The building was to have year round usage, with a particular emphasis on conference business in the summer months when the building would need to cope with high internal gains. A number of heating and cooling strategies were explored but the team eventually settled for an integrated slab heating/cooling system linked via a heat

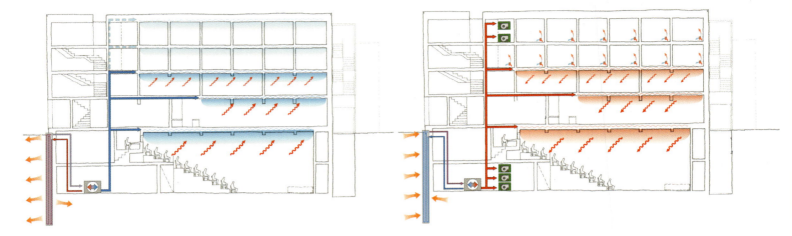

pump to a geothermal energy storage system, comprising pipe loops built into the building piles. The heat pump would be located in the basement and no additional heat rejection equipment would be necessary at roof level, thus eliminating the potential planning issues with such an arrangement. The slab-integrated pipework got rid of the ceiling voids and ultimately helped make room for the additional floor of accommodation.

The building is designed to exemplary thermal insulation standards, following on from the performance of Constable Terrace at UEA and the ARCO Building at Keble. All of the rooms are constructed to be airtight when windows are closed and have balanced ventilation systems with integral heat recovery. Glazed areas are controlled and the main glass facade to the courtyard faces to the east. Further energy reduction measures included a perimeter displacement ventilation system to the auditorium and seminar rooms, which are supplied from high performance heat recovery units incorporating an indirect evaporative ('adiabatic') cooling component for the summer months. The resulting air quality is exceptional, in the auditorium especially.

The most unusual feature of the systems in the building however is the geothermal heating and cooling system, which uses the structural piles as heat storage devices. The substantial lower ground floor contains pipe loops that conduct heat either from the ground in winter or into the ground in summer. The pipe loops are connected to a reversible heat pump in the basement, which can heat or cool as desired. The great benefit of the arrangement is that the relatively stable ground temperature makes heat collection and rejection considerably more efficient than other means and leads to much lower energy consumption.

The limited ceiling void space available also led to a complete re-think of the drainage strategy to eliminate the vertical drainage stacks. The building is fitted with a vacuum drainage system that uses small bore horizontal drainage pipes to lift the waste water away from appliances and convey it to the vertical risers at each end of the building in

Sloane Robinson Building, Keble College. The geothermal piles use the earth as a heat sink thus reducing energy use in the building. In effect the earth serves to heat the building in winter and cool it in the summer for massive long-term cost saving.

a manner familiar on ships, aircraft and more recently, trains. The further benefit of this arrangement is that water consumption from WC flushing is reduced by 60 per cent.

So, necessity as the mother of invention or a logical design morphosis? In a way this project represented a bit of both, the response to height restrictions triggering design solutions that might otherwise not have emerged but are nonetheless valid. The value to the client of the additional floor of accommodation was particularly significant and was calculated to merit the complexity and additional cost that resulted.

Years after the completion of this building, geothermal energy solutions are being recognised as the next big thing by many environmental designers. As regulatory requirements continue to increase, and the inclusion of renewable energy sources becomes an intrinsic and regulated element of all major projects, the benefits of geothermal type solutions will become increasingly evident. This building led the way.

It was in the development of the designs for the Ashmolean Museum in Oxford and the Virginia Museum of Fine Art (VMFA) in Richmond, Virginia, USA that our work with Rick Mather Architects moved onto a different scale and complexity. The environment of galleries as abstract space is all about light and air, these are the prime sensations before the art takes hold. Some art, of course, has very particular environmental requirements, some less.

Both are complex extensions to existing buildings, the Ashmolean being particularly complicated in the way that it will be stitched onto the back of the existing museum buildings. Both have rigorous controls of floor to floor levels established by existing gallery floor levels and both aspired to add significantly more space than might at first seem possible within the constraints of the site.

The specific requirements of the curatorial briefs represented a considerably more rigorous environmental challenge than were required by any of the earlier projects. At atelier ten we were in the throes of completing the Baltic Centre for Contemporary

Arts in Gateshead at the time that the design work on the Ashmolean started, and so had some experience of the issues involved in dealing with gallery conditions and the highly variable loads to which they are subjected.

Our researches for both of the projects caused us to look at many twentieth century galleries and the way in which the architects had dealt with light and air in particular. Two architects were of particular influence, Louis Kahn and Renzo Piano. Kahn for his projects at the Kimbell and at Yale, where the Yale Art Gallery and the Mellon Center for British Art are representative of his work at both ends of his career. His oft quoted words "I hate ducts, I hate them thoroughly, but because I hate them so thoroughly, I feel they have to be given their place. If I just hated them and took no care, I think that they would invade the building and completely destroy it…" resonate through the projects, not necessarily because Rick Mather hates ducts, just because he likes to keep them under control and know where they are and what they do.

The two projects started at almost the same time in our office but they followed very different trajectories through the design stages. However, it is true to say that the research and development that we undertook on each project informed the other.

In both cases the fundraising process heavily influenced the programme and progress of the design work. The Ashmolean in particular followed the start/stop programme that is typical of Lottery funded projects with brief periods of intense activity followed by long periods of waiting for good news. We and the museum were fortunate that the good news ultimately came but there was a considerable further delay while matching funding was secured.

In Virginia the fundraising seemed to be less of a problem, although Rick Mather worked hard with trustees in the early days of the project to ensure confidence in the design. The programme here was complicated by the approvals process for any project receiving State funding. This process resulted in a hiatus of up to six months between work stages as non-standard design solutions were interrogated by State employees and value engineered. Both of these processes test the continuity and resolve of a design team but the concepts for both of the museums were sufficiently robust and ingrained in the scheme to survive them.

The most significant design decision in the early part of both projects was to condition the galleries using a displacement approach rather than the more conventional mixing air delivery system that is common in older museums. We had used the technique successfully at the Earth Centre, the Baltic Centre and at Federation Square in Melbourne (which was still under construction at the time) and Renzo Piano had employed it in a number of galleries including the Menil Gallery in Houston and the Beyeler in Basle.

This method also has the benefit of maintaining the art in very stable conditions and there are significant energy cost benefits when maintaining controlled environments, particularly when combined with high performance heat recovery systems. Integration is, however, much more complex and imposes a significant degree of rigour on the whole design team. Having already used displacement ventilation on several previous projects, Rick Mather Architects recognised the potential of it, particularly in terms of removing ductwork from ceiling voids, the consequent effect on floor to floor heights and access requirements and, most importantly for us, the significantly reduced energy consumption. By organising the galleries around a series of vertical distribution shafts they could be conditioned from the top down and the space saved by the absence of ceiling voids allowed an additional floor of galleries to be constructed.

Our commitment to the concept was to be tested in depth on the Virginia Museum of Fine Art project. One of the first things that we did was to tour the existing museum, which extends over 107,000 square metres (351,000 square feet). We looked at the systems that they were familiar with and discussed with curators, facilities and the Museum management group what worked and what was less successful. The overall impression was of huge amounts of void space in the section that did contain a great deal of ductwork and other equipment, but even more, empty space. We saw the constructed empty voids as wasted space, certainly Mather did, and determined that we could improve on this apparent inefficiency in our design for the extension. We also saw very inefficient existing systems and determined to bring the client's operational team and our associate engineers, Hankins and Anderson, with us in the decision.

Rick Mather's advocacy for the solution continued and when we made a joint presentation to the Expansion Committee in Richmond during the schematic design it was championed as the only logical way to condition a modern gallery (which I have to say I am convinced to be the case). Once we had convinced the conservation staff and trustees that it was the right way to go it only remained to bring the facilities (engineering) team to a number of successful museums: Tate Modern, Baltic and the Great Court at the British Museum and, just to prove that the laws of physics applied equally on the other side of the Atlantic, to Renzo Piano's Menil Gallery in Houston which had been 'displacing' very satisfactorily since 1984.

This broad approval was followed by an exhaustive Computational Fluid Dynamics (CFD) study of the galleries and of the large atrium that links the old and new gallery spaces. Despite the fact that the system had broad acceptance worldwide as an appropriate one for fine art galleries there remained some sceptics. In the galleries the CFD modelling was used to validate the proposed layouts and to test the positioning and range of various outlet diffusers before we completed and signed off on the proposition to our partner engineers in the USA. Rick Mather Architects and the then Museum Director, Michael Brand, were also keen to avoid the floor diffusers that are a feature of the Menil, Tate Modern and Beyeler galleries. They preferred them to be unseen in a shadow gap slot between wall and floor and the CFD modelling allowed us to validate the airflow and distribution with this arrangement.

The client was also interested in knowing the likely conditions of the walls of the main atrium, which will become the principal circulation route through the museum, and we were concerned about temperatures on the bridges that link the various levels of the museum through the atrium. The modelling allowed us to prove that the space was suitable for many types of installation.

Ashmolean Museum, Oxford. Displacement ventilation is being used at both the Ashmolean Museum and the Virginia Museum of Fine Arts. Fresh air is introduced at floor level and slowly rises through the space as it becomes polluted and is extracted at high level. The diagrams show interlocking double-height gallery arrangement at the Ashmolean Museum with their 'thick' service walls.

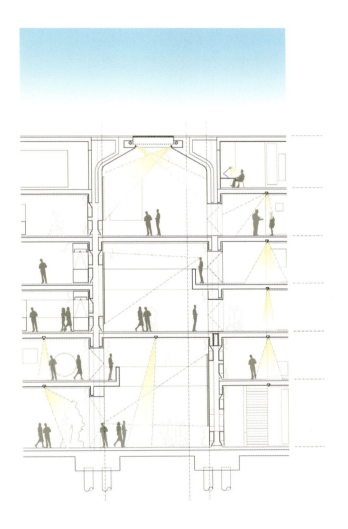
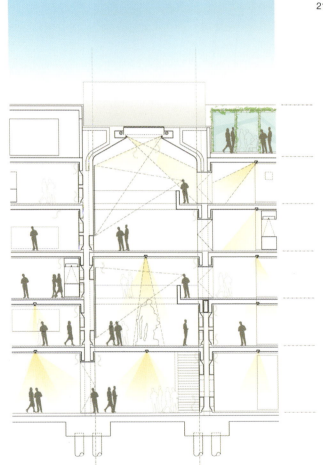

Architecturally the air distribution system placed quite significant constraints on the layouts and these took considerable negotiation and integration. The system is based around vertical ducts that are routed on the gridlines at a spacing of six metres. This sets up the grid of the galleries and ultimately generates the framework around which all of the fixed gallery spaces are planned. This is where we get to the 'Kahnian' moment as every vertical had to be understood in terms of its origin at roof level or basement level and it's destination on one of the five main floors of gallery space.

Inevitably with projects of this size, development and integration of the air distribution network is just one of many design conversations that go on. Others relating to things like glazing, shading, and daylighting of the restoration workshop are equally dynamic and interactive as processes with most discussions leading to the appropriate refinement of the design. It is, however, true to say that the complete integration of the gallery conditioning system has the most fundamental effect on the layout and organisation of the building, but not in a way that negatively compromises flexibility— rather it provides a framework for considerable future flexibility.

It was during the hiatus following submission of the Schematic Design Stage for the VMFA that the Ashmolean Museum received its lottery funding and we began to develop the detailed design for this equally large but very different project.

The concept was already in place to use the displacement system from the early design stages, but it had to be rigorously tested and approved by the University of Oxford's engineers before it could be adopted for the scheme. With this building we developed a series of so-called 'fat-walls' that run from the rooftop mechanical room right through the building. These carry the air to each of the floors in individual ducts and provide the length of wall for the shadow gap distribution arrangement described previously. The walls were established at an early stage to link all of the galleries together and provide concealed vertical routes to and from every space to roof level. They have remained a robust but outwardly invisible element of the design throughout its development. A mock up in a testing laboratory in Finland allowed the proposal to be tried, with some

surprising results—a narrowing of the shadow gap to 75 millimetres (three inches), for example, actually improved the air distribution.

It would be wrong of me to leave the reader with the impression that the development and integration of these strategies was an entirely problem free process. Rick Mather and his team have a talent for reduction; like creating a fine bouillon from a large pan of stock—all of the superfluous fluids are boiled off. So it is with the centimetres and millimetres of air distribution slots and ducts and conduits, and the trick is not to allow it to be reduced too much. This is the essence of the Rick Mather Architects product, refined and spare but nonetheless rich for that.

Sloane Robinson Building, Keble College. One of the heat exchange coils being wrapped around a pile reinforcement to create a geothermal pile.

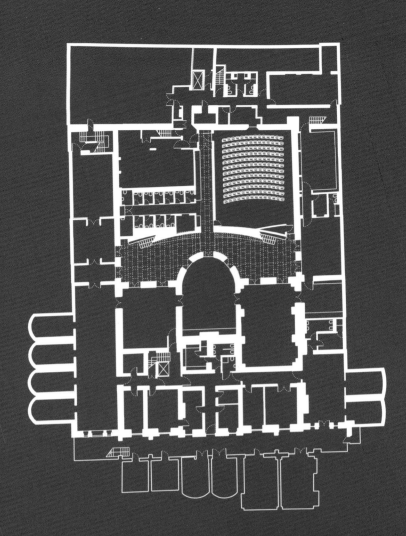

Timeline

1973–1974 **Beale Apartment**
Swiss Cottage, London
A renovation and extension
of a duplex, with new
mezzanine, roof garden and
skylights.

1967 **Espoo Competition**
Helsinki, Finland
Third prize in the
international competition
for the design of a new
city of 350,000, and its
city centre organised
around a new river valley
park—with Don Genasci.

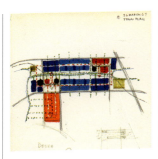

1976 **African Continental Bank**
Moorgate, London
A project for a modern banking
hall and offices, in a 1920s
office building.

216   000   001   002   010   017   018   044   049

1977 **'They Came to London' Exhibition**
Art Net Gallery, London

1975 **The George Hotel**
Lambourne, Berkshire
A project for a new
restaurant and bar, with
a residence above, in this
horse racing village.

1970 **Taylor Residence**
Sissinghurst, Kent
A renovation of a sixteenth
century house; interiors
are stripped back to
restore the beautiful
original rooms.

1973–1976 **Peter Eaton Antiquarian Bookshop**
Holland Park, London
A new building with an all-glass street front,
double-height from the roof lights down to
basement. The clients' existing apartment
above was retained.

1967 **Taylor Dental Surgery**
Tunbridge Wells, Kent
A minimal interior, with
all equipment concealed
behind built in cabinets.

1973 **Practice Established**
Camden Town, London

1971–1972 **Architect's House**
Camden Town, London
An extension and renovation of a terrace
house with roof garden on top—the
kitchen/dining room is on a mezzanine
below, overlooking the living room, the
bedrooms are in the middle, and the
studio at street and basement levels.

1977–1978 Architect's House and Studio
Belsize Park, London
The top two floors are rebuilt to form a large living space, with a mezzanine opening out to roof garden. The studio is on the street and garden levels.

1979–1981 House for Two Psychiatrists
Chalk Farm, London
A renovation and replanning of an 1840s classical villa with bedrooms below the living room. A new mezzanine and roof terrace were built above, and consulting rooms added at the garden level.

1977–1984 Architectural Association
Bedford Square, London
The AA school and club, in three large Georgian town houses, were renovated and replanned to provide a new gallery, lecture hall, bookshop, slide library, bar and reception. Construction was phased over five summers.

1980–1981 Seligmann Apartment
London

1977–1979 New House For Guy Gladwell
Kentish Town, London
A high north lit painting studio overlooks a double-height living room, angled south towards the sun and a view down a long narrow garden. Bedrooms and a roof garden are on top.

1980 Dean and Curtin Dental Surgery
London

1981 Varley Residence Project
Ludford, Lincolnshire
A project for a modern house on the site of a razed country house. All rooms face south to the sun and view. Guest rooms are stacked in a tower that terminates the entrance drive. The surviving game larder and gateway are incorporated into a new entrance court behind.

1982–1984 The Venue
A project for a multilevel club in a disused cinema.

1984–1986 Grange Walk Studios
Bermondsey, London
An abandoned Victorian school is developed as apartments, facing a new courtyard defined by a new terrace of houses, on the corner of an inner city site.

1987 Latif Apartment
St Paul's, London
A 1950s apartment is opened up into one continuous space, divided by new units that house essential functions.

218   138 139   145 151 155   165   184   188 191   201

1981–1993 Latif Residential Estate and Water Garden
Khartoum, Sudan

1987 'Four London Architects' Exhibition
9H Gallery, London

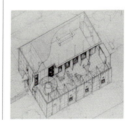

1985 Sports Pavilion Project
University of East Anglia, Norwich
A project for a restaurant and terrace overlooking the sports fields, raised above the new changing rooms.

1981 Vauxhall Cross Competition
London
A project for offices and houses around squares under a reinstated eighteenth century pleasure garden—with Mark Guard.

1983–1985 Science Park Project
University of East Anglia, Norwich

1981–1982 Schools of Education and Information Studies
University of East Anglia, Norwich
The new construction opens up the undeveloped north side of campus. The schools focus on a large landscaped courtyard. Routes through the buildings cross a triple-height space providing central reference. Complex bridges connect through Lasdun's 'teaching wall' to the campus beyond.

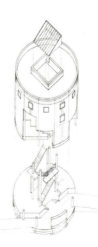

1983–1985 Climatic Research Unit
University of East Anglia, Norwich
A late addition to the brief for the new Schools of Education and Information Studies, housed in a cylindrical 'gatehouse' in front.

1985–1986 Saatchi Renovation
St John's Wood, London
A project for house renovation, to incorporate improved gallery space and living area.

1986–1989 Dworkin Residence
Belgravia, London
A remodelled Georgian town house with a double-height glazed dining room giving on to the garden, overlooked by the living room. Bedrooms are above and below, and a large study and terrace are on the top floor.

1987 Halkin House Competition
Belgravia, London
A project to convert and extend a parking garage into a luxury hotel.

202   205   208   211   216   231   236   219

1986–1988 51,51 Restaurant
Brompton Cross, London
An abandoned street level space is stripped out under a 1930s apartment building, and extended out into a courtyard under a saw-tooth glass roof, for a new restaurant.

1986–1988 Wychcombe Studios
Belsize Park, London
Mezzanines are added to a Victorian studio on either side of the restored double-height space. A high north window is at one end, and a new ply spiral stair at the other, leading up to a pyramidal glass room over two new en suite bedrooms.

1986–1987 Zen Central
Mayfair, London
The restaurant is opened to the street and extended to the full depth of this disused post office. The wall curves back to make space for a black glass bar. The new carpet, chairs, tables and stools were designed by Rick Mather Architects.

1985–1986 ZeNW3
Hampstead, London
This was the first in the series of Zen restaurants. The restaurant opens to the street through a new glass facade. Two floors are united by a roof-lit double-height space. A new bar is built behind a marble slab. There is a waterfall down the stair balustrade. Carpet, tables and chairs were designed by Rick Mather Architects.

1988–1989 Zen
Hong Kong
A massive concrete structure supporting a 35 storey hotel above contrasts with the glass 'water dragon', wood panelling, polished plaster and etched glass in this 500 seat restaurant.

1989–1992 Hoffmann House
Hampstead, London
1994 RIBA National Award
1994 RIBA Regional Award

1988 'Correspondences Paris—Londres' Exhibition
Institut Français d'Architecture, Paris and Lille

1988 South Quay Station
Isle of Dogs, London
A project for a space below an elevated light rail station, with shops and a restaurant.

220   239   247   257   261   271   277   283   288

1988 University of East Anglia Masterplan
Norwich
A 25 year expansion plan for new buildings and a new entrance route.

1987–1988 Point West Kensington
South Kensington, London
A redundant 1960s office block was transformed into 450 apartments and new build penthouses. The new tower penthouse includes an indoor swimming pool with underwater porthole views over London, and a series of roof gardens.

1989–1992 The Times Newspaper Headquarters
Wapping, London
1992 RIBA Regional Award
1992 Breeam Award

1988–1989 Ma & Pa Restaurant
Whetstone, London
An all glass front maximises light and views into this long narrow restaurant, with mirrors to doubling its apparent width. The bespoke chairs, tables and bar were designed by Rick Mather Architects.

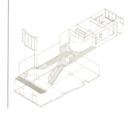

1988 Waddington Art Gallery
Cork Street, London
The floor at the front was removed to give light and views to the basement sculpture gallery. An entrance bridges across to the stair suspended from cables.

1990 **Zen Montreal**
Montreal, Canada
A new restaurant below the Four Seasons Hotel. The long curved wall with mirrors above creates the illusion of additional space. The freestanding glass tiled oval bar and bespoke furnishing were designed by Rick Mather Architects.

1992–1995 **ARCO Building**
Keble College, Oxford
1996 RIBA Award
1996 British Construction Industry Award
1997 Civic Trust Award

1991–1993 **Constable Terrace and Nelson Court**
University of East Anglia, Norwich
1994 RIBA Award (Constable Terrace)
1995 Civic Trust Award (Constable Terrace)

1993 **University of Westminster Masterplan Competition**
Regent Street, London
Winning scheme.

1991–1993 **Neal's Yard Penthouse**
Covent Garden, London

290   302   309   313   320/321   322   329   343   346   349   221

1992 **Urban Approaches Monograph and Zen Restaurants Books**

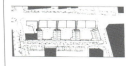

1993 **De Montfort University Student Residence Competition**
Leicester
Winning scheme.

1993 **'Glass Heat and Light: The Work of Rick Mather Architects' Exhibition**
Architecture Foundation, London

1991–1993 **Drama Studio**
University of East Anglia, Norwich
The flexible seating for 200 allows for any configuration. The foyer, rehearsal room and adjacent outdoor area are also useable as performance spaces.

1990–1991 **Now & Zen**
Covent Garden, London
The use of advanced and innovative techniques of glazing in the facade and the pavement made it possible to bring light and the 'theatre of the street' into the three floors of the restaurant. The structural glass front includes the first frameless glass revolving door ever built. A 'glass dragon' waterfall drops through three floors from the roof to the basement. The mirror at back continues the free form of the mezzanine. Furnishing is by Rick Mather Architects.

1995–1997 **The Priory**
Hampstead, London
1997 AIA UK Excellence in Design Award
1998 RIBA Award
1998 Civic Trust Award

1994–2000 **The Wallace Collection**
Manchester Square, London

1994 **Phillips Restaurant**
Redhill, Surrey
Views are controlled by windows opening to the terrace and gardens. A grid of trees under roof lights gives a sense of the garden running through the dining area.

1994 **BRE Offices Competition**
Garston, Watford
Finalist.

1995 **@venue Restaurant**
St James', London

222 354 358 360 363 364 365 368 370 372 373 377

1995–1998 **ISMA Centre**
University of Reading
1999 RIBA Award
1999 Civic Trust Award

1995–2002 **Sloane Robinson Building**
Keble College, Oxford
2003 Building of the Year Best Public Building Brick Award
2003 Oxford Preservation Trust Environmental Award
2004 RIBA Award
2005 Civic Trust Award (commendation)

1994 **Yoshinos Restaurant**
Piccadilly, London
This pub was remodelled into a Japanese restaurant and sushi bar.

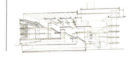

1994 **Tate Bankside Competition**
London
Finalist.

1994 **Lycée School Competition**
South Kensington, London
This was the competition-winning project for a new gateway building with gymnasium and classrooms.

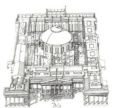

1994 **British Museum Great Court Competition**
Bloomsbury, London
Rick Mather Architects won second place in this international competition. A simple, lightweight glass roof encloses the courtyard as an exhibition area and link to the back. Two stairs curve up around the reading room to a new roof terrace and down to the new basements, so that all the extensive collection could be stored and displayed on site.

1996 Royal Horticultlural Society
Westminster, London
The first scheme for an alternative site on Vincent Square.

1995–1999 Dulwich Picture Gallery
London
2001 AIA Business Week/Architectural Record Award
2001 RIBA Award
2001 RIBA Crown Estate Conservation Award
2002 Civic Trust Award

1997–1998 National Youth Centre for the Performing Arts Competition
Gloucester
This was a competition-winning project to transform a nineteenth century dock complex into residences, teaching and recording facilities, and a new auditorium. An outdoor performance space is located between the existing warehouses and the new building, with views across the dock to the existing Inland Waterways Museum.

1996–1997 Gower Building
University of Southampton

1999 Tent Project
The Dairy, Waddeson

1997–2001 Royal Horticultural Society
Westminster, London

1996–1999 Zepler Building
University of Southampton

1996–2020 University of Southampton Masterplan
Highfield Campus, University of Southampton

1996 Gallery of Scottish Art and Design Competition
Glasgow

1995–1998 National Maritime Museum
Greenwich, London
2000 Civic Trust Award

1997–2004 **Lyric Theatre**
Hammersmith, London
Competition winning scheme.

2001 **Pepys Building**
Greenwich, London

1998–1999 **Urvois House**
Holland Park, London

1998–2002 **Greenwich Landscape Masterplan**
London

224   411   412   413   414   416   423   424   428   429/430   433

1996–1999 **Homes for the Future**
Glasgow Green, Glasgow
2000 Regeneration of Scotland Award
2002 Civic Trust Award

2000–2001 **Mirazur Restaurant**
Menton, Côte d'Azur, France
with Larsson & Kope J Architects and
Grassi Architetto

1999–2008 **Ashmolean Museum Expansion**
Oxford

1999 **Drill Hall Theatre Competition**
London
This was the winning project on a tight urban site for the construction of a new 350 seat theatre and arts centre behind an existing nineteenth century facade. The complex is arranged around a central skylit atrium.

1998 **Riverside Apartment Complex**
Rochester
A regeneration project, carefully integrated into the historic waterfront. It includes 200 river view apartments organised around a square.

1998–2000 **Technology Tower**
London Metropolitan University
The smooth shape counterpoints the adjacent 1960s tower. At the top the boardroom opens onto a roof terrace.
2000 Islington Council Conservation Award

2000 Maritime Museum Competition
Genoa, Italy
Rick Mather Architects were awarded second place for the renovation and extension of these waterfront medieval warehouses—with Vittorio Grassi.

2001–2007 Stowe School Masterplan
Buckinghamshire
A competition-winning scheme for the education zone within this historic country house and garden. The new buildings define linked garden courtyards.

2001–2008 Virginia Museum of Fine Arts Expansion
Richmond, Virginia, USA
2004 MIPIM/Architectural Review Future Projects Award

2001–2004 Jubilee Sports Centre
University of Southampton
Competition winning scheme.

2002–2010 Residential Quarter
Central Milton Keynes

2002–2003 Lincoln School of Architecture
University of Lincoln

2000 Sheffield One Competition
Sheffield
Rick Mather Architects were awarded second place for a regeneration plan for the city centre.

2002 Darwin Centre Competition
Natural History Museum, London
Finalist.

1999– South Bank Centre Masterplan
London

2001 University of Lincoln Masterplan Competition
University of Lincoln
Winning scheme.

2000 Horsebridge Masterplan Competition
Whitstable
This project for the regeneration of the town centre and waterfront with a new square art gallery and performance facilities, incorporating residential and commercial accommodation, was awarded second place.

2002–2027 Natural History Museum Masterplan
London
58,000 sqm (624,000 sqft) new build potential was identified for the expansion and renewal of existing facilities, plus the restoration of Waterhouse's Grade I listed complex.

2003–2004 Coking Works Masterplan
Chesterfield

2000 Galleria Sabauda Masterplan
Turin, Italy
This was the winning scheme for relocationg a collection to a remodelled and restored Manica Nuova, a wing of the Royal Palace—with architects Grassi, OBR and Albini.

226 468 471 472 475 478 480   481 483

2003–2004 Parkhill Masterplan Strategy
Sheffield

2003 Derby Quad Competition
Derby
Rick Mather Architects were finalists for a new cinema and arts complex in the city centre.

2004–2009 Lincoln Arts Centre Competition
University of Lincoln
The winning scheme for a performance space, cinemas, gallery and restaurant.

1997–2007 St Clare's College Masterplan Competition
Oxford
Winning scheme.

2003–2007 Eastbourne Cultural Centre Competition
Eastbourne
Winning scheme.

2005–2007 Student Residence
Stowe School, Buckinghamshire
New student residence for 144 girls,
adjacent to Lorimer Chapel.

2005 Liverpool John Moores University Masterplan
Liverpool

2005–2006 East Greenwich Masterplan
London
A winning scheme for a new residential
quarter and civic hub, linking historic
Greenwich with the new development
around the Dome.

484   488   490   492   493 494 495   497   500

2006 Rick Mather Architects Book
London

2005 The Queen's College Competition
Oxford
A competition to design a library
extension beneath the Provost's Garden.

2006 Byrom Street Campus Masterplan
Liverpool John Moores University.

2005–2008 Liverpool John Moores
University Design Academy Competition
Liverpool
Winning scheme.

2005–2007 Barking Masterplan
London
A masterplan for the regeneration of
a central urban block, with mixed-use
residential buildings around a new market
square.

488 Ville Reale di Monza Competition
Italy
The practice won second prize in this
international competition to refurbish
the whole villa and its gardens—with
architects Grassi, OBR and Albini.

Selected Bibliography
Colleagues and Consultants
Index

Selected Bibliography

General

Ajmone, Giulia, Cristina Ruiz and Martin Bailey, "Rick Mather times 3", *Art Newspaper*, May 1997

Blume, Mary, "A visionary architect with designs on the past", *International Herald Tribune*, 28–29 July 2001

Croft, Catherine, "Rick'll fix it", *Building Design*, 2 June 2000

Fallowell, Duncan, "Zen and the art of buildings", *Financial Times*, 19 February 2000

Gibson, Grant, "Held In reserve", *Blueprint*, April 2004

Glancey, Jonathan, "The ship of things to come", *The Guardian*, 31 May 1999

Irving, Mark, "Rick Mather", *Blueprint*, June 1999

Johnson, Paul, "London's new chamber of horrors and three success stories", *Spectator*, 5 April 2001

Mather, Rick, "Architect's approach to Architecture", *RIBA Transactions 6*, January 1984

Niesewawnd, Nonnie, "Tales from the capital's riverbank", *The Independent*, 21 February 2000

Pearce, David, "Virgin Architect", *Blueprint*, June 1984

Powell, Kenneth, "The sympathetic modernist", *Sunday Telegraph*, 26 March 2000

Rozhon, Tracie, "An American expatriate sheds light on London", *New York Times*, 5 April 2001

Worsley, Giles, "The galleries of London seen with fresh eyes", *New York Times*, 7 January 2001

Hoffmann House, Hampstead, London

"Glass Structure—Private House", *Architects' Journal*, July 1992

Goodman, Pamela, "A house of its own", *House & Garden*, April 1993

Maxwell, Robert, "Enlightenment", *RIBA Journal*, November 1997

McGuire, Penny, "Heart of Glass", *Architectural Review*, February 1993

Sustainable Residential Quarter, Central Milton Keynes

Gardiner, Stephen, "Encouraging schemes at Milton Keynes", *The Times*, 4 October 2004

Rose, Steve, "Urban Outfitters", *The Guardian*, 15 July 2004

Lyric Theatre, Hammersmith, London

Gibson, Grant, "Lyric presents its new look", Blueprint, 1 April 2004

Pearman, Hugh, "How to make an entrance", *The Sunday Times*, 15 March 2004

Lincoln School of Architecture

Gardiner, Stephen, "New seat of learning in a dazzling sea of white", *The Times*, 24 November 2003

Maxwell, Robert, "Campus Creation", *Architecture Today*, 1 January 2004

South Bank Centre Masterplan, London

Alberge, Dalya, "South Bank to have £150m facelift", *The Times*, 18 February 2000

Booth, Robert, "Rick Mather's South Bank plan wins early plaudits", *Architects' Journal*, 17 February 2000

Brookes, Richard, "Architects want to bury South Bank under a hill", *The Sunday Times*, 26 December 1999

Fallowell, Duncan, "Zen and the art of buildings", *Financial Times*, 19 February 2000

Hattersley, Lia, "Mather unveils South Bank", *Building Design*, 18 February 2000

Hoge, Warren, "A concrete Arts bunker on the Thames awaits the kiss of life", *The New York Times*, 3 June 1999

Iduhu, Ogale, "Longside bankside development project seeks to revive dormant arts centre", *Wall Street Journal*, 18 February 2000

Iloniemi, Laura, "Mather's plan adds human touch to brutal South Bank", *Architectural Record*, November 2000

Jenkins, Simon, "The South Bank sails into the future", *Evening Standard*, 17 February 2000

Moss, Stephen, "Master Builder", *The Guardian*, 18 February 2000

Pearman, Hugh, "Squaring the South Bank circle", *The Sunday Times*, 20 February 2000

Powell, Kenneth, "Complex Solution", *RIBA Journal*, March 2000

Worsley, Giles, "Mather may come up with a winner", *Daily Telegraph*, 18 February 2000

Neals Yard Penthouse, Covent Garden, London

Izzo, Ferruccio, "Apartment in London", *Domus*, April 1995

Dulwich Picture Gallery, London

Binney, Marcus, "Reframed Glass", *The Times*, 23 May 2000

Cruikshank, Dan, "La prima galleria d'arte (The first art gallery)", *Domus*, October 2000

Czarnecki, John E, "Expressing the art of good business", *Architectural Record*, 1 October 2001

Davey, Peter, "Spirit of Soane", *Architectural Review*, August 2000

Harbison, Robert, "Light Touch—Mather at Soane's Dulwich", *Architecture Today*, July 2000

Ashmolean Museum, Oxford

Talt, Simon, "The Ashmolean prepares to punch its weight", *The Times*, April 2004

Worsley, Giles, "Heroic collections find a worthy setting", *Daily Telegraph*, 8 November 2005

Virginia Museum of Fine Arts, Richmond, USA

Goodheart, Adam, "In Richmond, a museum aims for the big league", *New York Times*, 23 April 2003

The Wallace Collection, London

Darley, Gillian, "New Faces", *Royal Academy Magazine*, Summer 2000

Keleney, Guy, "Victoria wins the lottery", *The Independent*, 21 June 2000

Mallett, Lee, "Blowing the dust off a hidden jewel", *Building Design*, 6 May 1995

Spring, Martin, "Art Explosion", *Building*, 26 May 2000

Stockley, Philipa, "Summer on a plate", *Evening Standard*, 21 June 2000

The National Maritime Museum, Greenwich, London

Bevan, Robert, "Behold the sea", *Building Design*, 23 April 1999

Brownlie, Keith, "Naval glazing", *Architects' Journal*, 6 May 1999

Gordon, Jacqueline, "The National Maritime Museum, Greenwich", *Access By Design*, Summer 1999

Jammers, Judith, "Ein Amerikaner, der britischer als eim brite zu werke geht", *Gewerbeimmobilien*, 22 September 2000

Pearman, Hugh, "In a glass of its own", *The Sunday Times*, 21 March 1999

Worsley, Giles, "A modern answer to a classic problem", *Daily Telegraph*, 24 March 1999

ARCO Building, Keble College, Oxford

Hammett, Michael, "All you need to know about bricking it", *Building Design*, 26 May 2000

Slessor, Catherine, "Keble connection", *Architectural Review*, September 1995

Welsh, John, "Brick Layers", *RIBA Journal*, September 1995

The Priory, Hampstead, London

Kirwan-Taylor, Helen, "Design Solutions—Exposure", *House & Garden*, April 2000

Malfatti, Patrizia, "Spazi di vetro (Glass spaces)", *Abitare*, October 1999

Maxwell, Robert, "Enlightenment", *RIBA Journal*, November 1997

Moonan, Wendy, "Blueprint—Life in prism", *House & Garden* (USA), May 2001

Niesewand, Nonnie, "It's in London and it's a lovely white house on a hill (but not as you'd imagine it)", *The Independent*, 11 December 1997

University of East Anglia, Norwich

Dormer, Peter, "Hallmarks of quality on the campus", *The Independent*, 8 December 1993

"Lessons in low energy", *CIBSE Journal*, June 1992

Miller, John, "Nuovi edifice nel campus della university of East Anglia", *Casabella*, May 1987

Swenarton, Mark, "Energy—Warm space, cool, aesthetic: Rick Mather @ UEA", *Architecture Today*, February 1994

Welsh, John, "Student Union", *RIBA Journal*, February 2004

Now & Zen Restaurant, London

Blasco, Berta, "Restaurante Now & Zen—Una revision de los primeros modernos", *Diseno Interior*, September 1991

Dawson, Susan, "Zen and the art of glazing", *AJ Focus*, April 1991

Green, Emily, "Zen and the art of cool", *The Independent*, 23 February 1991

Gardner, Carl, "Zen and the art of restaurant design", *RIBA Journal*, July 1991

Henderson, Justin, "A Zen dragon", *Interiors* (USA), April 1992

Williams, Gaynor, "Through the looking glass", *Interior Design*, April 1991

"Zen—order die kunst mit Strabchen zu essen", *Baumeister*, January 1992

ISMA, University of Reading

Cadji, Miríam, "Brick Bond", *RIBA Journal*, June 1999

Cargill Thompson, Jessica, "Different Class", *Building*, 15 May 1998

Times Headquarters Building, London

Pearman, Hugh, "Zen at Work", *Blueprint*, October 1991

Recent Colleagues and Consultants include:

Gavin Miller, Stuart Cade, Peter Culley, Chris Wood, Noor Abdul Aziz, Stala Antoniades, Juliet Aston, Tom Bagley, Emma Coulson, Alney Dalley, Peter Dean, Kevin Fellingham, David Finlay, Clinton Grobler, Riaan Hahndiek, Nick Hill, Ben Hyett, Adam Jundi, Richard Keep, Valerie Kuster, Pablo Lazo, Marie Annick Le Blanc, Jacqui Levi, Janice Maclennan, Simone Marchesi, Alejandro Martinez, Paul Mullin, Sabine Nakanishi, David Nightingale, John O' Shea, Tim Paul, Luke Pearson, Javier Rada Domingo, Joachim Reiter, Alison Rigby, Susan Russell, Lee Schmidtchen, Nina Scholtz, Richard Sharp, Fiona Sheppard, Luis Treviño, Zelda van Wyk, Dojanne Vermeulen, Andy Wakefield, David Watson, Matthew Wickens, Dumrong Wongprayoon.

Albini Architetti. All Clear Design. Arup. Atelier 10. Buro Happold. Connell Mott Macdonald. David Bonnett. Davis Langdon. David Goodwin. Dewhurst MacFarlane + Partners. DPA. Eckersley O' Callaghan. FISEC. Alexandre Garcin. Gardiner and Theobald. Ghibaudo Architectes. Gifford + Partners. Gross Max. Hankins + Anderson. HRW . Margaret Pope. Mark Guard Architects. David John. John Philips Planning Consultancy. Larsson & Kopaj Architectes. L'Observatoire. Opinion Leader Research. Land Use Consultants. Ken Lovett. MACE. Malcolm Chard Associates. Metaphor. Michael Edwards + Associates. Mouchel Parkman. Mouvement & Paysages. Nitty Gritty. OBR Architetti. Olin Partnership. Plincke Landscape. Sandy Brown Associates. Robert Maguire. Space Syntax. SMBW Architects. Theatreplan. Thornton Firkin + Partners. Turner + Townsend. Grassi Architetto. WhitbyBird. Georgie Wolton.

Past Colleagues and Consultants include:

Douglas McIntosh, Elena Acciari, Kevin Allsop, Mark Annen, Stephen Archer, David Ardill, Alan Arnstein, Christopher Bagot, Charles Barclay, Helen Barry, Neil Bennett, Ulrich Blum, Ann Bodkin, Juan Gonzalez, Tim Carter, Amarjit Chaggar, Hazel Charik, John Cockings, Marge Collins, Jim Conti, Malcolm Cormack, Holly-Anne Coward, Tom Coward, Jean Michel Crehaz, Tom Croft, Jason Curtis, Huw Davies, Jim Davis, Dusan Decermic, Tom Deckker, Michael Delaney, Tim Dodd, Karen Elliott, Charles Emberson, Glyn Emrys, Dan Evans, Michael Foster, Anne French, Edward Finnamore, Dominique Gagnon, Edgar Gonzalez, Andrew Goodenough, Graham Goymour, Vittorio Grassi, Bill Greensmith, Mark Gregg, Mark Guard, Steph Hamilton, Nicky Hawkins, Ian Hay, Richard Jeffery, Russell Owen Jones, Steve Joyce, David Kelly, Stephen Keyser, Kaly Khela, Pete Kiernan, Judy Koetter, Nicolas Laurent, Susan Le Good, Richard Lindley, Graham Livesly, Pascal Madoc Jones, Sean Mahon, Fiona Marr, Annie Martin, Christopher Mascal, Melody Mason, James McGrath, Matthew McGrory, Ken McKay, Gary McLuskey, Melissa Merryweather, Guillermo Millacet, Ian Mongomerie, Neil Morton, Dan Naegele, David Naessens, Ashima Narang, Antoinette O'Neil, Terrance O'Neil, Brian O'Tuama, Laura Parker, John Parker, James Parritt, Kathie Peacock, Wong Tak Ping, Chris Proctor, Will Pryce, Michael Regan, Penny Richards, Leandro Rotondi, Peter Roy, Aya Ruppin, Florence Salberter, Mustafa Salman, David Selby, Riko Sibbe, James Slade, Malcolm Smith, Tom Smith, Dan Smith, Roberto Eduardo Spada, Rebekah Staveley, Tom Teggin, Luke Thurman, Carolyn Trevor, Paul Tuppeny, Derek Tynan, Tom Verebes, Damon Webb, Ken Wilder, Iain Williams, Chris Wisdom, Voon Yee Wong, Tom Young.

Alan Baxter + Associates. Andrew Reid + Partners. Atelier One. Atelier 75. BDP. Berkeley Consultancy. Blyth + Blyth. Bucknall Austin. Ward Cole. Fulcrum Consulting. Don Genasci. Helix. Peter Henderson. Trevor Hollinger. Ian White Associates. Jean Florino. Jenkins + Potter. Murray John. John Vincent. Koetter Kim. Lighting Design Partnership. Marshall Botting Associates. Gordon Marshall. Mendick Waring. Pentagram. Price + Myers. Malcolm Reading. Alex Ritchie. Robert Jackson Associates. John Seaman. Matthew Wells. West 8. Zisman Bowyer + Partners.

Index

51,51: 219
9H Gallery: 218
@venue Restaurant: 160–162, 203–204, 222
African Continental Bank: 216
Ahrends Burton and Koralek: 205
Architect's House extension and renovation: 216
Architect's House and Studio: 217
Architectural Association: 12, 52, 116, 217
The Architectural Record: 199
ARCO Building, Keble College: 5, 16–21, 142–143, 205, 206, 221
Arts and Crafts: 41
Ashmolean Museum: 13, 52, 72–77, 201, 205, 207, 208, 210–211, 212–213, 224
Association of Consulting Engineers: 139
atelier ten: 208

Baltic Centre for Contemporary Arts: 207, 209, 210
Bank Stock Office, John Soane: 149
Barking Masterplan: 227
The Bartlett School of Architecture: 182
Bath: 15
Beale Apartment: 216
Bellew, Patrick: 197 ff.
Beyeler Gallery, Renzo Piano: 209, 210
Bilbao: 16
Bloomsbury: 15
Bodker, Chris: 204
Boyarsky, Alvin: 12
Brand, Michael: 210

BRE Offices Competition: 222
British Film Institute: 98
British Museum Great Court Competition: 222
Brown, Capability: 96
Burlington Villa, Chiswick: 14
Butterfield, William: 16, 17, 18, 20, 205
Byrom Street Campus Masterplan: 227

Cambridge: 13
Carrier, Willis: 199
Carter, Pat: 35, 184, 187, 204
Casa del Fascio, Giuseppe Terragni: 166
Chester: 14
Climatic Research Unit, University of East Anglia: 87, 116
Cockerell, Charles Robert: 13, 72, 74, 175
Codes of Practice: 185, 186, 193
Coking Works Masterplan, Chesterfield: 96–97, 226
Compostela: 50
Congress Theatre: 166, 171, 173
Connell, Ward & Lucas: 41
Constable Terrace, University of East Anglia: 114–115, 116–125, 195, 200, 206, 221
'Correspondences Paris—Londres' Exhibition: 220
Côte d'Azur: 161, 163–165
Cutty Sark: 55

Darwin Centre Competition: 225
De Montfort University Student Residence Competition: 221
Dean and Curtin Dental Surgery: 217
Derby Quad Competition: 226
Docklands Light Railway: 55
Drama Studio, University of East Anglia: 116–117, 221
Drill Hall Theatre Competition: 224
Dulwich College, John Soane: 150–151
Dulwich Picture Gallery: 52, 78–85, 148–149, 150–151, 152–153, 195, 223
Dworkin Residence: 219

Earth Centre: 209
East Greenwich Masterplan: 227

East Midlands Development Agency: 96
Eastbourne Cultural Centre: 170–173, 226
Eisenman, Peter: 50, 174
English Partnerships: 96, 128
Escher, MC: 48
Espoo Competition: 216
Evans, Sir Arthur: 72, 74

FA Firman: 187
Federation Square, Melbourne: 209
Festival of Britain: 100
Ford, Andy: 200
Foster, Norman: 87, 116, 203
'Four London Architects' Exhibition: 218
Fourth Duke of Manchester: 62
Fry, Maxwell: 41
Fulcrum Engineering: 189, 200

Galleria Sabauda Masterplan: 226
Gallery of Scottish Art and Design Competition: 223
Gehry, Frank: 16, 51
Genaschi, Don: 216
The George Hotel: 216
Georgian: 41, 52
Glasbau Hahn: 189
Glasgow Year of Architecture, 1999: 132
'Glass Heat and Light: The Work of Rick Mather Architects' Exhibition: 221
Gower Building, University of Southampton: 86, 88–89, 223
Le Grand Verre, La Villette, Peter Rice: 182
Grange Walk Studios: 218
Great Court, British Museum: 210
Greenwich Landscape Masterplan: 110–113, 224
Greenwich Visitor Orientation Centre: 110
Greenwich World Heritage Site: 110–111
Gross. Max. Landscape Architects: 102
Guard, Mark: 218

Halkin House Competition: 219

Hampstead: 32, 40–49
Hankins and Anderson: 210
Hardwick, Sir Philip: 59
Hawksmoor, Nicholas: 56–57
Hayward Gallery: 98, 102–103
'Hellfire Plan', Ashmolean Museum: 74
Hertford House: 62
Hodgson, John: 187
Hoffmann, Lord and Lady: 187
Hoffmann House: 32–35, 182, 187–191, 193, 194, 220
Homes for the Future: 130–133, 224
Horsebridge Masterplan Competition: 225
House for Two Psychiatrists: 217
Hunt, Anthony: 181

ISMA Centre, University of Reading: 138–141, 222

Jacoby, Helmut: 128–129
Jencks, Charles: 12
Jones, Inigo: 56–57
Jubilee Gardens: 98, 100–101, 102
Jubilee Sports Complex, University of Southampton: 88–91, 225

Kahn, Louis: 175, 208, 212
Keble College: 13, 16–23, 84, 128, 142, 205
Kent, William: 96
Kimbell Gallery, Louis Kahn: 208
Kip, Johannes: 110
Koolhaas, Rem: 50, 146, 174

Lampugnani, Vittorio: 15–16
Lasdun, Denys: 87, 116, 218
Latif Apartment: 218
Latif Residential Estate and Water Garden: 218
Le Corbusier: 36, 41, 47, 146, 174
Libeskind, Daniel: 15, 50, 174
Lincoln Arts Centre: 30–31, 226
Lincoln Cathedral: 25, 27
Lindley Library: 66–67, 70–71
Lissitzky, El: 48
Liverpool John Moores University Design Academy: 6–7, 92–95, 176, 227
Liverpool John Moores University

Masterplan: 227
Livingstone, Ken: 14
Llewelyn Davies and Weeks: 128
Lloyd Wright, Frank: 199
London Eye: 98
Los Angeles: 128
Lovett, Ken: 205
Lutyens, Edward: 55, 175
Lycée School Competition: 222
Lyric Theatre Hammersmith: 166–169, 224

Ma & Pa Restaurant: 180–181, 220
Macfarlane, Tim: 35, 177 ff.
Maison Cook, Le Corbusier: 47
Manchester House: 62
Manhattan: 14
Mannerism: 142, 144, 146, 149, 150, 151, 166, 174, 175
Mannerism, John Shearman: 151
Mannerism and Modern Architecture, Colin Rowe: 146
Maritime Museum Competition: 225
Marks' Standard Handbook for Engineers: 186
Meier, Richard: 51
Mellon Center for British Art, Yale University, Louis Kahn: 208
Menil Gallery, Renzo Piano: 209, 210
Metropolitan Roman Catholic Cathedral, Liverpool: 92–95
Michelangelo: 152
Mirazur Restaurant: 161, 163–165, 177, 224
Modern Movement: 20, 174
Modernism: 30, 36, 41, 79, 142, 144, 149, 181, 182, 203
Morphosis: 51
Museum of the Moving Image: 98

National Film Theatre: 98
National Gallery: 55, 149
National Maritime Museum: 52, 53–61, 84, 110, 112, 223
National Theatre: 98
National Youth Centre for the Performing Arts Competition: 223
Natural History Museum: 52, 110, 226
Neal's Yard Penthouse: 36–39, 221
Nelson Court, University of East Anglia: 116–117, 121, 125–127
Neo-classicism: 59, 149
New House for Guy Gladwell: 217
New York Times: 174
Now & Zen Restaurant: 182–187, 188–189, 200, 221

Old Heath and Hampstead Society: 41
'Old Royal Naval College, Christopher Wren and Nicholas Hawksmoor: 56–57, 110, 112
Oxford: 13, 16–23

Paris: 47
Parkhill Masterplan Strategy: 226
Pearman, Hugh: 166
Pepys Building: 110, 112, 224
Peter Eaton Antiquarian Bookshop: 116, 216
Phillips Restaurant: 222
Piano, Renzo: 208, 209, 210
Pitzhanger Manor, John Soane: 149
Point West Kensington: 220
Postmodernism: 47, 174
Price, Cedric: 139
Prince Charles, Prince of Wales: 62
The Priory: 11, 40–49, 146–147, 155, 175, 201–202, 203, 222
Pugin's Palace: 14
Purcell Room: 98, 102

The Queen's College Competition: 227
Queen Elizabeth Hall: 98, 102
Queen's House, Inigo Jones: 56–57, 110

Raphael: 152
Residential Quarter Central Milton Keynes: 128–130, 225
Rice, Peter: 181, 182
Riverside Apartment Complex: 224
van der Rohe, Mies: 48
Royal Festival Hall: 98, 100, 102
Royal Horticultural Society: 52, 66–71, 146–149, 223
Royal Institute of British Architects: 50, 203
Rowe, Colin: 146

Rozhon, Tracie: 174

Saatchi Renovation: 219
Sainsbury Centre, University of East Anglia, Norman Foster: 87, 116, 200
Samuel & Harding: 41
Samuelly, Felix: 181
Schools of Education and Information Studies, University of East Anglia: 218
Science Park Project, University of East Anglia: 218
Seligmann Apartment: 217
Shearman, John: 151, 152
Sheffield One Competition: 225
Sloane Robinson Building, Keble College: 16–23, 142, 144, 206, 213, 222
Soane, John: 79, 82–83, 84–85, 149, 150–151, 175
Soane Museum: 149
South Bank Centre Masterplan: 98–103, 225
South Bank Centre Urban Design Strategy: 100
South Quay Station: 220
Spence, Sir Basil: 86
Spitalfields: 14
Sports Pavilion Project, University of East Anglia: 218
St Clare's College Masterplan Competition: 226
St Giles Chapel, Oxford: 18
St John Wilson, Colin: 16
Stirling, James: 81
Stirling Prize: 203
Stowe School Masterplan Competition: 225
Student Residence, Stowe School: 227

Tate Bankside Competition: 222
Tate Modern: 210
Taylor Dental Surgery: 216
Taylor Residence: 216
Technology Tower: 224
Ten Books on Architecture, Vitruvius: 203
Tent Project: 223
Terragni, Giuseppe: 166, 174

The Times Newspaper Headquarters: 134–137, 142, 175, 220
'They Came to London' Exhibition: 216
Towner Art Gallery: 166, 171
Turner, JMW: 25
Tyrell, C: 79

University of East Anglia: 11, 87, 114–127, 195, 200, 206, 220
University of Lincoln Masterplan: 25–31, 142, 225
University of Lincoln School of Architecture: 11, 12, 25–31, 144–145, 225
University of Reading: 138–141
University of Southampton Masterplan: 86–91, 223
University of Westminster Masterplan Competition: 221
Urvois House: 154–159, 224

Varley Residence Project: 218
Vauxhall Cross Competition: 218
Venturi, Robert: 149, 175
The Venue: 218
Villa Savoye, Le Corbusier: 36, 146
Villa Stein, Le Corbusier: 146
Ville Reale di Monza Competition: 227
Virginia Museum of Fine Arts: 12, 104–111, 191–193, 207, 209–212, 225
Vitruvius: 203

Waddington Art Gallery: 220
The Wallace Collection: 52, 62–67, 222
Wren, Christopher: 56–57
Wychcombe Studios: 219

Yale Art Gallery, Louis Kahn: 208
Yoshinos Restaurant: 222

Zen, Hong Kong: 220
Zen Central: 219
Zen Montreal: 221
ZeNW3: 32, 33, 161, 219
Zepler Building, University of Southampton: 86, 88–89, 223

Acknowledgements and Picture Credits

We would like to thank all of our clients, without whom the projects would not have been realised. A special thanks to the team in the office whose research and organisation have made this book possible, led by Matthew Wickens with Valerie Kuster, re-drawing of plans and sections by Nina Scholz, Luke Pearson, Fiona Sheppard, Adam Jundi and Ana Serrano. We would also like to thank Duncan McCorquodale of Black Dog Publishing for working with us to produce the book.

Finally, a big thank you to the graphic designer, Karen Willcox.

Arcaid/Richard Bryant 10, 32(l,r), 40, 41, 42, 44–45, 46, 49, 52, 78, 84, 85, 138, 139, 147, 148(b), 149, 153, 180, 183, 185, 201, 217, 219, 220, 221. David Churchill 133. Enrico Cano 163, 164, 165, 177. Keith Collie 20, 23, 142, 156, 158(t), 198. Chris Gascoigne 33, 34, 35(t,b). Dennis Gilbert 21, 36, 37, 38, 61, 114, 119(l,r), 122, 124, 134, 137, 141(l,r), 157, 189, 221. Jason Hawkes 111. Keith Hunter 131, 151. Ian Lambot 220. John Linden 160, 161, 162. Benedict Luxmoore 82, 90(t,b), 154, 158(b), 159, 167, 168(t). Peter Mackinven 64, 65. James Morris 24, 27, 28, 53, 60, 66, 68, 70, 71, 89(l,r), 144, 145. Pro Photo 4, 19. Andrew Putler 106. Andreas Schmidt 204. Sealand Aerial Photography 31, 117, 170. Frank Walter 143. Andrew Weekes 12

Ashmolean Museum 72, 74(t). Dulwich Picture Gallery 78, 150. Keble College 16. National Maritime Museum 57, 112. Oaker 6–7, 93, 95, 129(b), 171, 173. Lincolnshire County Council 25. Virtual Artworks 101-103.

Unless otherwise stated all greyscale drawings are 1:500.

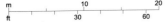

Black Dog Publishing
Architecture Art Design Fashion History
Photography Theory and Things

© 2006 Black Dog Publishing Limited, the architects and authors. All rights reserved

Texts by Robert Maxwell, Patrick Bellew and Tim Macfarlane

Designed by aleatoria

Black Dog Publishing Limited
Unit 4.4 Tea Building
56 Shoreditch High Street
London
E1 6JJ

Tel: +44 (0)20 7613 1922
Fax: +44 (0)20 7613 1944
Email: info@bdp.demon.co.uk
www.bdpworld.com

All opinions expressed within this publication are those of the authors and not necessarily of the publisher.

British Library Cataloguing-in-Publication Data.

A CIP record for this book is available from the British Library.

ISBN 1 904772 38 2

All rights reserved. No part of this publication may be reproduced, stored in a retrieval system, or transmitted, in any form or by any means, electronic, mechanical, photocopying, recording, or otherwise, without prior permission of the publisher.

Every effort has been made to trace the copyright holders, but if any have been inadvertently overlooked the publishers will be pleased to make the necessary arrangements at the first opportunity.